Canadian Phonics

On the cover, a busy street
With lots of friends for you to meet.
Turtle's truck comes to a stop
As Beaver comes out from a shop.
Spider's skateboard whizzes by
As Kitty waves her hand up high.

Now look closely everywhere
To find some letters hiding there.
If you can, then look around
For pictures of words that make each sound.

gage EDUCATIONAL PUBLISHING COMPANY

© 1999 Gage Education Publishing Company
1120 Birchmount Road, Toronto, Ontario M1K 5G4
www.nelson.com

All rights reserved. No part of this publication may be reproduced, stored in a retrieval system, or transmitted, in any form or by any means, without the prior written consent of the publisher or a licence from the Canadian Copyright Licensing Agency (Access Copyright). For Access Copyright licence, visit www.accesscopyright.ca or call toll-free to 1-800-893-5777.

Adapted from material developed, designed and copyrighted by Steck-Vaughn

Acknowledgments

5 "I Love Pets" by Lori Newman from *Inside Myself* by the Newfoundland Library Association. Courtesy of Lori Newman. / 21 "The Maple Tree" by Dennis Lee from *Jelly Belly* (Macmillan of Canada, 1983). © 1983 Dennis Lee. With permission of the author. / 39 "Crunching My Lunch" from *Toes in My Nose* by Sheree Fitch. © 1987 Sheree Fitch. Reprinted with permission of Doubleday Canada Ltd. / 56 "Just Because" from *An Armadillo is Not a Pillow* by Lois Simmie. / 73 "General Store" from *Taxis and Toadstools* by Rachel Field. © 1926 Rachel Field. Used by permission of Bantam Doubleday Dell Books for Young Readers. / 91 "To Catch a Fish" by Eloise Greenfield. © 1988 Eloise Greenfield. Used by permission of HarperCollins Publishers. / 127 "Friends" from *Mischief City* by Tim Wynne-Jones. © 1986 Tim Wynne-Jones. Used by permission of Groundwood/Douglas & McIntyre Children's Books.

Photography by Digital Studios, Austin, Texas and Park Street Photography with the following exceptions:
The stock agencies have been abbreviated as follows.

AA: Animals Animals; C: Corbis; GH: Grant Heilman Photography, Inc.; IW: The Image Works; PE: PhotoEdit; PR: Photo Researchers; SB: Stock Boston; SM: The Stock Market; SS: Superstock; TI: Tony Stone International; UN: Uniphoto; US: Unicorn Stock Photos.

(ambulance) © Dr. A. Farquhar/Alan Photos; (ant) © Runk/Schoenberger/GH; (antler) ©Leonard Lee/TI; (astronaut) Canadian Space Agency; (baby) © SS; (beach) © Jeff Gnass/SM; (bee) © Stephen Dalton/AA; (bird) © Arthur Smith III/GH; (boat) ©Bachmann/PR; (boy) © Tony Latham/TI; (bridge) © UN; (bug) © Roy Morsch/SM; (bunny) © Stephen Green Armitage/SM; (bus) ; (cat); (cheek) © SS; (chick) © Tim Davis/TI; (children) © Kevin Cavanagh/PR; (chimney) © Tony Freeman/PE; (chin) © Eric Bemdt/US; (city) © Province of British Columbia; (claw) © Tom McHugh/PR; (cloud) © Craig Tuttle/SM; (clown) © SS; (crab) © Bruce Forster/TI; (cricket) © Gilbert S. Grant/PR; (cry) © Tom McCarthy/SM; (dad) © Jon Feingersh/SM; (day) © SS; (deer) © PhotoDisc; (dive) © David Madison/TI; (drink) © UN; (drive) © David Wright/UN; (duck) © Robert Maier/AA; (dune) © SS; (elephant) © James Balog/TI; (engine) © Berle Chemey/UN; (exercise) © Bao Cao/Explorer/PR; (fang) © C.W. Schwartz/AA; (fence) © William Manning/SM; (fin) © Fred McConnaughey/PR; (fire) © PE; (fish) © Fred McConnaughey/PR; (fly) © Donald Specker/AA; (fox) © Darrell/Fulin/TI; (frog) © Tom Brakefield/SM; (fry) © Felicia Martin/PE; (fuse) © V. Wilkinson/Valan Photos; (gate) © Robert W. Ginn/UN; (giraffe) © Zefa/SM; (girl) © SS; (goat) © James Marshall/SM; (golfer) © Joe McBride/TI; (grass) © Randa Bishop/UN; (hay) © Tony Craddock/TI; (heel) © Spencer Grant/PE; (hide) © Tony Freeman/PE; (hill) © Michael Lustbader/PR; (home) © Robert Shafer/PE; (horse) © SS; (hut) © Margo Moss/US; (igloo) © David Roseberg/TI; (iguana) © Zigmund Leszczynski/AA; (ill) © Michael Newman/PE; (instruments) © PhotoDisc; (jay) © Michael Bisceglie/AA; (jet) © Ross Harrison/TI; (jog) © Bruno Maso/PR; (judge) © Dennis MacDonald/US; (jump) © David Young Wolff/PE; (keg) © Michael & Barbara Reed/AA; (kick) © Bob Thomas/TI; (kiss) © Michael Newman/PE; (kitchen) © Willie Hill/FPG; (kitten) © SS; (lady) © UN; (lake) © Scott Melcer; (lamb) © Henry Auloos/AA; (leash) © Mary Kate Denny/PE; (lion) © PhotoDisc; (lip) © David Young-Wolff/PE; (lizard) © PhotoDisc; (map) © Nora Good/Masterfile; (man) © SS; (mask, medal) © PhotoDisc; (meet) © Michael Newman/PE; (melon) © John Kelly/TI; (men) © UN; (mice) © Rodger Jackman/AA; (money) © Kennan Cooke/Valan Photos; (moth) © Charles Krebs/SM; (mouse) © J. M. Labat/Jacana/PR; (mule) © Karen Holsinger Mullen/US; (nap) © SS; (noise) © Michael Newman/PE; (nose) © UN; (octopus) © D. Fleetham/AA; (ostrich) © SS; (otter) Patti Murray/AA; (ox) © Russell Grunake/US; (path) © Tom McCarthy/PE; (pay) © Sean O'Neill/Ivy Images; (peacock) © UN; (peek) © Frank Pedrick/IW; (piano) © Spencer Grant/PE; (plane) © Doris De Witt/TI; (puppy) © AA; (puppet) © Jeff Greenberg/US; (quack) © Mark Peterson/TI; (queen) © AP/WPA ROTA/Canapress; (quiet) © Photodisk; (rabbit, raccoon) © PhotoDisc; (rainbow) © Zefa/SM; (rat) © Robin Redfern/AA; (ray) © Stephen Studd/TI; (reach) © Laura Dwight/C; (read) © Ellen Senisi/IW; (road) © M. L. Sinibaldi/SM; (roof) © Larry Lefever/GH; (run) © Rich Baker/US; (sad) © Ken Cavanagh/PR; (sail) © Jim Brown/SM; (sea) © Bob Abraham/ SM; (seal) © Patti Murray/AA; (seed) © SS; (shark) © W. Gregory Brown/AA; (shave) © David Pollack/SM; (sheep) © Tim Davis/PR; (ship) © Harvey Lloyd/SM; (sing) © David Young-Wolff/PE; (sky) © Michael Busselle/TI; (sled) © Barbara Stitzer/PE; (sleep) © Myrleen Ferguson/PE; (slide) © Michael Newman/PE; (smell) © Roy Morsch/SM; (smile) © SS; (smoke) © Barry Rowland/TI; (snail) © Peter Steiner/SM; (snow) © Craig Tuttle/SM; (spot) © Renee Lynn/PR; (stop) © Michael Newman/PE; (submarine) © David Higgs/TI; (swan) © SS; (swim) © Kathy Ferguson/PE; (tail) © Otto Rogge/SM; (team) © Kaufman/SM; (television) © Rob Lewine/SM; (thorn) © Donald Specker/AA; (tiger) © PhotoDisc; (tree) © Rich Iwasaki/TI; (twins) © Chip Henderson/TI; (umpire) © Bonnie Kaminsky/PE; (use) © Bill Aron/PE; (vet) © Dimaggio/Kalish/SM; (volcano) © SS; (volleyball) © John Welzenbach/SM; (wait) © John Coletti/SB; (walrus) © SS; (wave) © Warren Bolster/TI; (web) © Tim Bach/TI; (weed) © Gabe Palmer/SM; (well) © Amy C. Etra/PE; (wet) © ChromoSohm/Sohm/US; (whale) © Gerald Lin/US; (wheat) © Kevin R. Morris/TI; (whiskers) © Chris Haigh/TI; (woman) © Photodisk; (worm) © Oxford Scientific Films/AA; (yard) © Robert Brenner/PE; (yawn) © Aneal Vohra/UN; (zoo) © Darleen Rotozinski; 5 © Y. Momatiuk/J. Eastcott/VALAN PHOTOS (boy with dog); © Malcolm Piers/The Image Bank (goldfish); 21 Kennan Cooke/VALAN PHOTOS (boy in tree); 39 © Jeff Speed/Canada in Stock/Ivy Images (child eating soup); 46 © Richard Hutchings/PhotoEdit; 56 A. Farquhas/VALAN PHOTOS; 73 © Steve Dunwell/The Image Bank; 91 © David Hanover/Tony Stone Images (boy with fishing pole, © Pat & Tom Leeson/Photo Researchers (trout); 127 © Bill Ivy (two children in silhouette); © Will Crocker/The Image Bank (Aladdin's lamp), © Daniel Arsenault/The Image Bank (robot).

Cover Design: Dave Murphy/Art Plus Ltd.
Cover Illustration: Jackie Snider

ISBN-13: **978-0-7715**-1029-8
ISBN-10: **0-7715**-1029-2
21 20
Printed and Bound in Canada.

Level A Contents

Unit 1   Consonants *m, d, f, g,* and Short Vowel *a*   Theme: Pets

Poem: *I Love Pets* by Lori Newman 5
Initial Consonants **m, d, f, g** 6
Initial **m, d, f, g** Review 10
Final Consonants **m, d, f, g** 11
Initial Short Vowel **a** 12
Medial Short Vowel **a** 13
Short Vowel **a** Phonograms 14

Spelling Short **a** Words 16
Reading Short **a** Words in Context 17
Writing Short **a** Words 18
Check-up Unit 1 19

Unit 2   Consonants *b, t, s, w,* and Short Vowel *o*   Theme: Outdoor Fun

Poem: *The Maple Tree* by Dennis Lee 21
Initial Consonants **b, t, s, w** 22
Initial **b, t, s, w** Review 26
Final Consonants **b, t, s** 28
Initial Short Vowel **o** 29
Short Vowel **o** 30
Short Vowel **o** Phonograms 31

Short Vowels **a, o** Review 33
Spelling Short **o** Words 34
Reading Short **o** Words in Context 35
Writing Short **o** Words 36
Check-up Unit 2 37

Unit 3   Consonants *k, j, p, n,* and Short Vowel *i*   Theme: What's for Lunch?

Poem: *Crunching My Lunch* by Sheree Fitch . . . 39
Initial Consonants **k, j, p, n** 40
Initial **k, j, p, n** Review 44
Final Consonants **k, p, n** 45
Initial Short Vowel **i** 46
Short Vowel **i** 47
Short Vowel **i** Phonograms 48

Short Vowels **a, o, i** Review 50
Spelling Short **i** Words 51
Reading Short **i** Words in Context 52
Writing Short **i** Words 53
Check-up Unit 3 54

Unit 4   Consonants *c, h, l, r,* and Short Vowel *u*   Theme: Off We Go!

Poem: *Just Because* by Lois Simmie 56
Initial Consonant **c, h, l, r** 57
Initial **c, h, l, r** Review 61
Initial Short Vowel **u** 63
Short Vowel **u** 64
Short Vowel **u** Phonograms 65
Short Vowels **a, o, i, u** Review 67

Spelling Short **u** Words 68
Reading Short **u** Words in Context 69
Writing Short **u** Words 70
Check-up Unit 4 71

Unit 5 — Consonants *v, y, z, qu, x* and Short Vowel *e*

Theme: At the Store

Poem: *General Store* by Rachel Field 73
Initial Consonant **v, y, z, qu** 74
Final Consonant **x** 78
Final Consonants **l, v, x** 79
Medial Consonants 80
Initial Short Vowel **e** 81
Short Vowel **e** 82
Short Vowel **e** Phonograms 83
Review Short Vowels **a, o, i, u, e** 85
Spelling Short **e** Words 86
Reading Short **e** Words in Context 87
Writing Short **e** Words 88
Check-up Unit 5 89

Unit 6 — Long Vowels

Theme: Adventures

Poem: *To Catch a Fish* by Eloise Greenfield ... 91
Long Vowel **a** 92
Long Vowel **a** Phonograms 94
Reading Long **a** Words in Context 95
Writing Long **a** Words 96
Long Vowel **o** 97
Long Vowel **o** Phonograms 99
Spelling Long **o** Words 101
Reading Long **o** Words in Context 102
Writing Long **o** Words 103
Long Vowel **i** 104
Long Vowel **i** Phonograms 105
Spelling Long **i** Words 107
Reading Long **i** Words in Context 108
Writing Long **i** Words 109
Long Vowel **u** 110
Long Vowel **u** Phonograms 112
Spelling Long **u** Words 114
Reading Long **u** Words in Context 115
Writing Long **u** Words 116
Long Vowel **e** 117
Long Vowel **e** Phonograms 119
Spelling Long **e** Words 121
Reading Long **e** Words in Context 122
Writing Long **e** Words 123
Final **y** as a Vowel 124
Check-up Unit 6 125

Unit 7 — Consonant Blends and Digraphs

Theme: Make-Believe

Poem: *Friends* by Tim Wynne-Jones 127
Initial Consonant Blends with **s** and **tw** ... 128
Initial Consonant Blends with **r** 130
Initial Consonant Blends with **l** 132
Reading Consonant Blends in Context 133
Consonant Blends Review 134
Initial Consonant Digraphs **ch, wh, th, sh** ... 135
Final Consonant Digraphs **sh, ck** 137
Final Consonant Digraphs **ng, nk** 138
Final Consonant Digraphs Review 139
Spelling Words with Consonant Blends and Digraphs 140
Reading Consonant Digraphs in Context ... 141
Writing Words with Consonant Blends and Digraphs 142
Check-up Unit 7 143

UNIT 1
Pets

Consonants m, d, f, g, and Short Vowel a

I Love Pets

Some pets I know
Are very small,
And some of them
Are very tall.
My dog is black.
My canary is yellow,
My fish is a very
funny fellow!

Lori Newman, Age 6
St. John's, Newfoundland

Think About It

What kinds of pets are small?
What animal would you like for a pet?

Write m if the picture name begins with the m sound.

m

mop

1. (coins)
2. (mitt)
3. (map)
4. (sun)
5. (mouse)
6. (dish)
7. (key)
8. (moon)
9. (fish)
10. (door)
11. (man)
12. (milk)

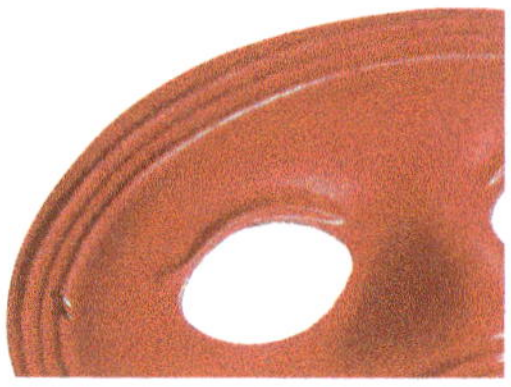

Unit 1: Initial Consonant *m*

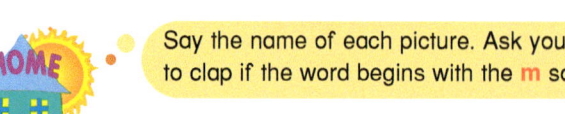

Say the name of each picture. Ask your child to clap if the word begins with the **m** sound.

Write d if the picture name begins with the d sound.

d

dog

1.
2.
3. d
4.
5.
6.
7.
8.
9.
10.
11.
12.

Ask your child to name three objects in your home that begin with the **d** sound.

AT HOME

Unit 1: Initial Consonant *d*

7

Write f if the picture name begins with the f sound.

 fan

f

1  f	2 	3 	4 
5 	6 	7 	8 
9 	10 	11 	12 

Unit 1: Initial Consonant *f*

AT HOME Take turns with your child naming pictures that begin with the **f** sound.

Write g if the picture name begins with the g sound.

gas

1	2	3	4

5	6	7	8

9	10	11	12

Ask your child to name three objects that begin with the g sound.

Unit 1: Initial Consonant *g*

Write a if you hear the short a sound in each picture name. Colour the pictures with the short a sound.

PHONICS and SPELLING

1. h a m
2. p _ n
3. c _ p
4. c _ t
5. n _ t
6. b _ g
7. l _ g
8. h _ t
9. m _ t

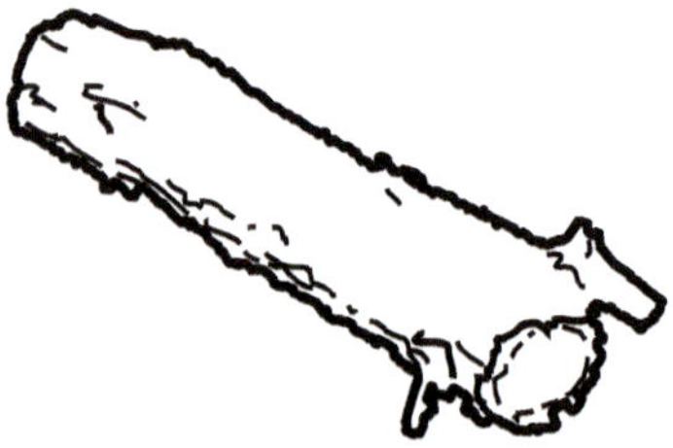

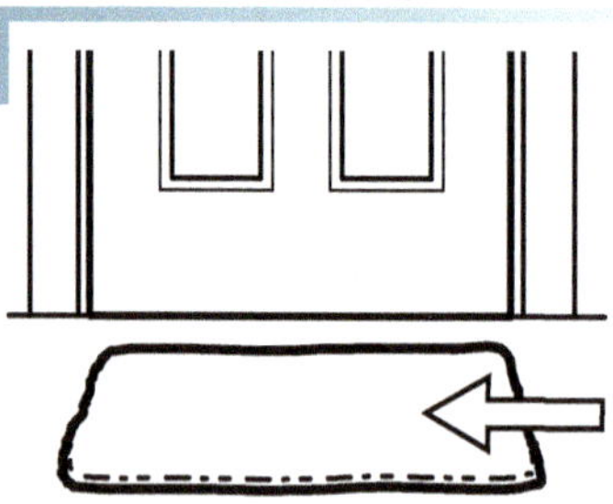

16 Unit 1: Spelling Short *a* Words

Look at the picture and read the sentence. Circle the word that completes the sentence. Write the word on the line.

1. Al and his ___dad___ get in a car.
   add (dad) sad

2. His dad has a _____.
   tap lap map

3. They buy some _____.
   gas bag has

4. They _____ to a pet shop.
   do go so

5. Al gets a pet _____.
   cat gas mask

6. The cat can run _____.
   mat fast bat

Point to a picture and have your child read the sentence that tells about it.

Unit 1: Reading **m, d, f, g,** and Short Vowel **a** in Context

17

Look at this picture of Sam the dog and Max the cat. Write about it. The words in the box may help you.

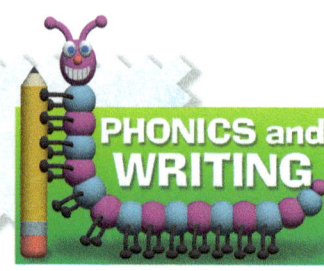

can
cat
fast
hat
pals
ran

Say the picture name. Write the letter that stands for the first sound.

Unit 1 CHECK-UP

m d f g a

1. 
2. 
3. 
4. 
5.
6. 
7. 
8. 
9. 
10. 
11. 
12. 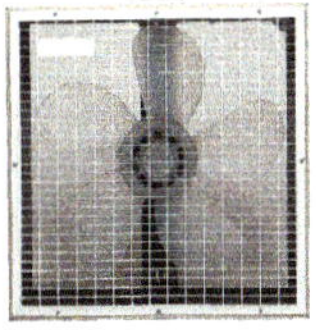
13. 
14. 
15.

Unit 1: Assessing Initial *m, d, f, g, a*

Unit 1 CHECK-UP

Say the picture name. Fill in the circle next to the letter for the last sound.

1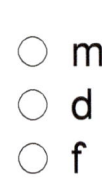
○ m
○ d
○ f

2
○ g
○ f
○ d

3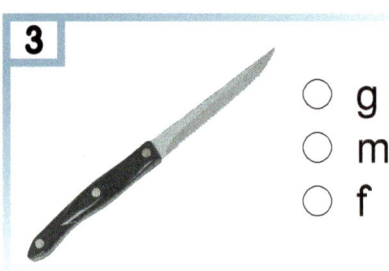
○ g
○ m
○ f

4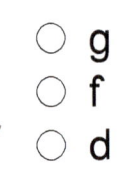
○ g
○ f
○ d

5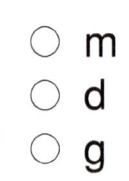
○ m
○ d
○ g

6
○ m
○ g
○ d

7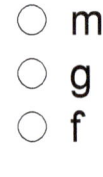
○ m
○ g
○ f

8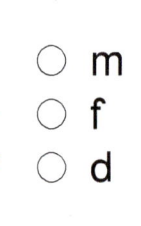
○ m
○ f
○ d

9
○ g
○ m
○ d

10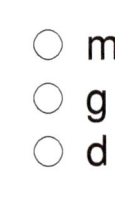
○ m
○ g
○ d

11
○ d
○ m
○ g

12
○ g
○ m
○ f

13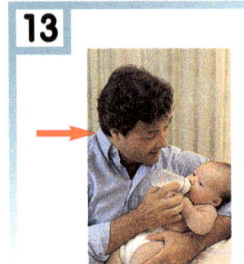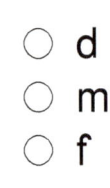
○ d
○ m
○ f

14
○ g
○ f
○ d

15
○ d
○ g
○ f

20 Unit 1: Assessing Final *m, d, f, g*

UNIT 2
Outdoor Fun

Consonants b, t, s, w, and Short Vowel o

The Maple Tree

My maple tree
Is neat to climb,
And there's a special
Branch of mine

Where I can perch
And not be seen,
And watch the world
Go by, and dream.

Dennis Lee

Think About It

What do you like to do outdoors?
What else is fun to climb?

Write b if the picture name begins with the b sound.

bus

1

2

3

4

5

6

7

8

9

10

11

12

Unit 2: Initial Consonant *b*

AT HOME

Say the name of each picture. Ask your child to pretend to toss a basketball into a basket if the word begins with the b sound.

Write t if the picture name begins with the t sound.

tire

t

1.

2.    t

3.

4.

5.

6.

7.

8.

9.

10.

11.

12.

AT HOME Say the name of each picture. Ask your child to tiptoe if the word begins with the t sound.

Unit 2: Initial Consonant *t*

Write s if the picture name begins with the s sound.

sock

s _____

1 	2 	3 	4 
5 	6 	7 	8 
9 	10 	11 	12 

Help your child name two pictures that begin with the s sound and then make up a sentence using the words.

Unit 2: Initial Consonant s

Say the name of each picture. Write the letter that stands for the **first** sound in each picture name.

Circle the letter that stands for the **last** sound. Then write the letter.

Write o if you hear the short o sound in each picture name. Colour the pictures with the short o sound.

PHONICS and SPELLING

1. t o p
2. d _ g
3. m _ t
4. g _ s
5. p _ p
6. b _ g
7. f _ x
8. h _ p
9. p _ t

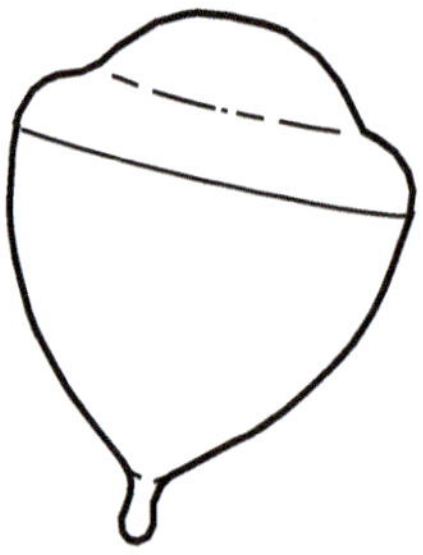

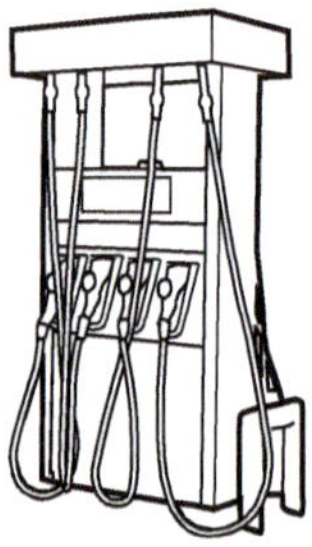

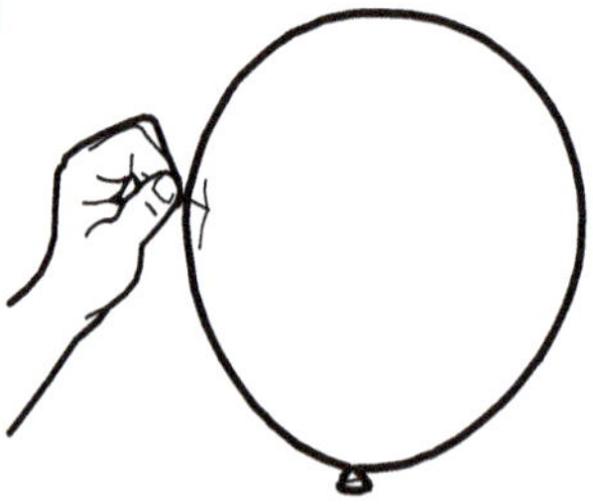

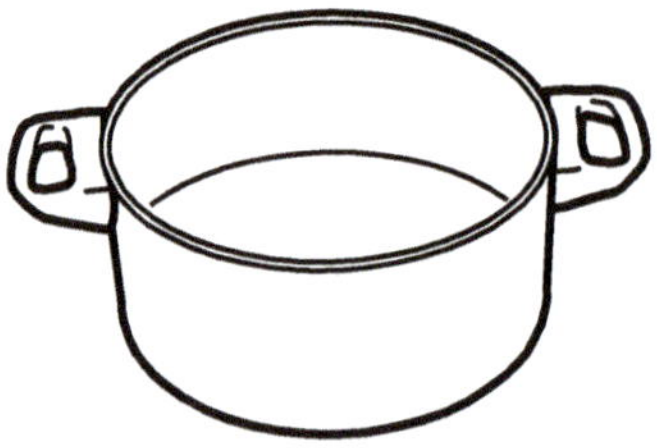

Unit 2: Spelling Short *o* Words

Look at the picture and read the sentence. Circle the word that completes the sentence. Write the word on the line.

1. Ann and __Tom__ go to a picnic.
   (Tom)   hot   dot

2. They eat _____ dogs.
   top   hot   hat

3. They _____ in big sacks.
   top   mop   hop

4. Tom likes to _____ the balls.
   toss   boss   fox

5. Tom won a toy _____.
   pot   dog   log

6. They like the picnic a _____.
   lad   lot   tot

Unit 2: Reading *b, t, s, w,* and Short Vowel *o* Words in Context

What do Bob and Dot see at the top of the hill? Write about it. The words in the box may help you.

| hop |
| log |
| off |
| rock |
| sock |
| top |

Say the picture name. Write the letter that stands for the first sound.

1 	2 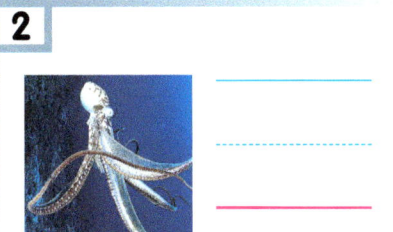	3 
4 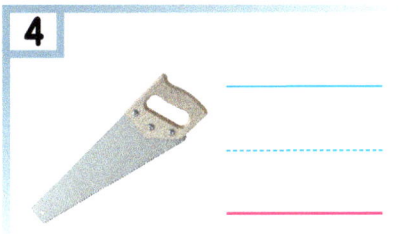	5 	6 
7 	8 	9 
10 	11 	12 
13 	14 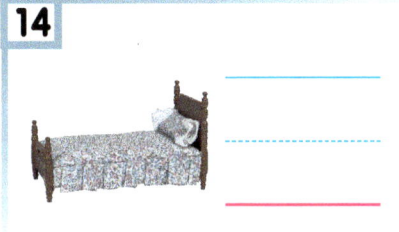	15 

Unit 2: Assessing Initial *b, t, s, w, o*

Unit 2 CHECK-UP

Say the picture name. Fill in the circle next to the letter that stands for the last sound.

b t s

1.
   ○ s
   ○ t
   ○ b

2.
   ○ b
   ○ t
   ○ s

3.
   ○ b
   ○ s
   ○ t

4.
   ○ b
   ○ t
   ○ s

5.
   ○ t
   ○ s
   ○ b

6.
   ○ s
   ○ b
   ○ t

7.
   ○ t
   ○ b
   ○ s

8.
   ○ t
   ○ s
   ○ b

9.
   ○ b
   ○ t
   ○ s

10.
    ○ t
    ○ s
    ○ b

11.
    ○ s
    ○ b
    ○ t

12.
    ○ t
    ○ b
    ○ s

13.
    ○ b
    ○ t
    ○ s

14.
    ○ s
    ○ b
    ○ t

15.
    ○ b
    ○ s
    ○ t

Unit 2: Assessing Final *b, t, s*

UNIT 3
What's for Lunch?

Consonants k, j, p, n, and Short Vowel i

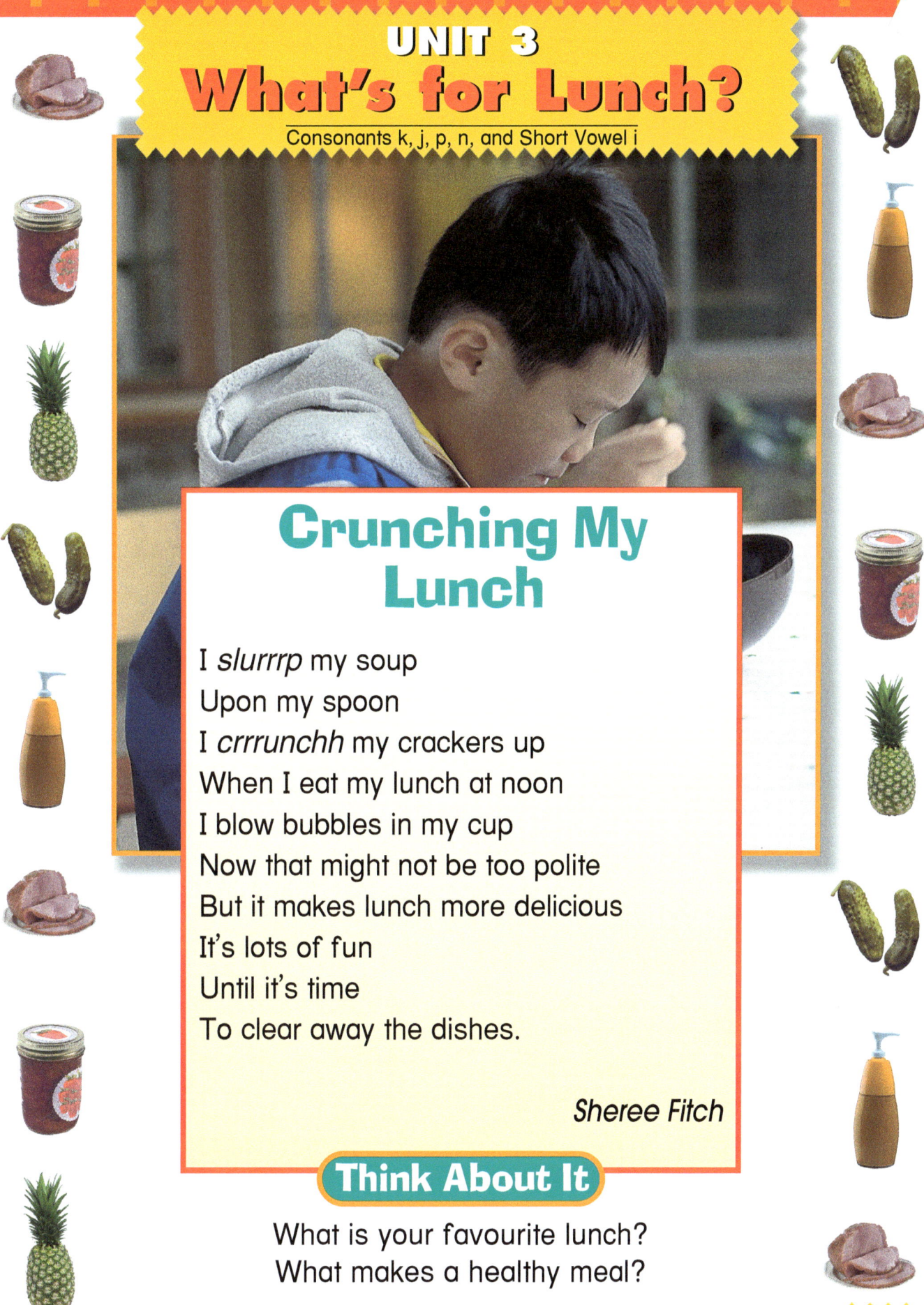

Crunching My Lunch

I *slurrrp* my soup
Upon my spoon
I *crrrunchh* my crackers up
When I eat my lunch at noon
I blow bubbles in my cup
Now that might not be too polite
But it makes lunch more delicious
It's lots of fun
Until it's time
To clear away the dishes.

Sheree Fitch

Think About It

What is your favourite lunch?
What makes a healthy meal?

Write k if the picture name begins with the k sound.

key

1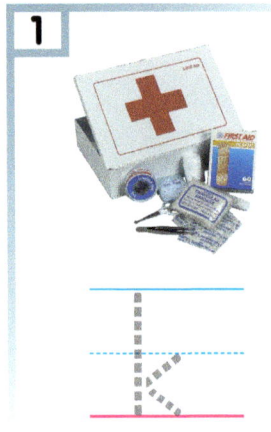

2

3

4

5

6

7

8

9

10

11

12

Say the name of each picture. Ask your child to pretend to kiss you if the word begins with the k sound.

Unit 3: Initial Consonant *k*

Write j if the picture name begins with the j sound.

jam

j

1	2	3	4

j

5	6	7	8

9	10	11	12

Say the name of each picture. Ask your child to jump if the word begins with the j sound.

Unit 3: Initial Consonant *j*

Write p if the picture name begins with the p sound.

p

pig

1
2 
3 
4

p

5 
6 
7 
8

9 
10 
11 
12

42 Unit 3: Initial Consonant *p*

Ask your child to complete the following sentence with a picture name that begins with the p sound: In Pam's purse is a ___.

Write n if the picture name begins with the n sound.

n̄ _____

nest

1	2	3	4
	n̄		

5	6	7	8

9	10	11	12

Say the name of each picture. Ask your child to nod if the word begins with the n sound.

AT HOME

Unit 3: Initial Consonant *n*

Say the name of each picture. Write the letter that stands for the **first** sound in each picture name.

k   j   p   n

1. kite
2. purse
3. jet
4. nuts
5. jacks
6. nine
7. kiss
8. pitcher
9. kangaroo
10. jacket
11. nest
12. peach

Unit 3: Initial **k, j, p, n** Review

Ask your child to name two pictures whose names begin with the same sound and to think of a sentence using both words.

What things would you give to a king? Write about it. The words in the box may help you.

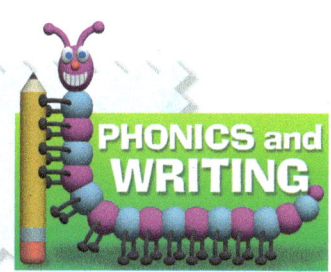

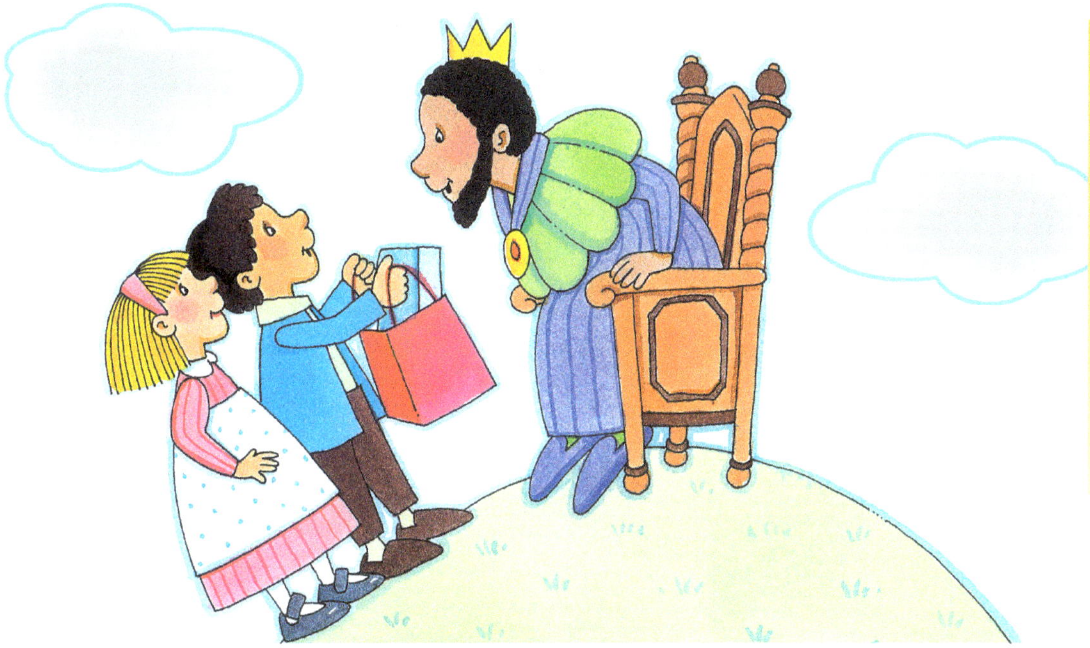

big
hill
his
kit
pig
will

Unit 3 CHECK-UP

Say the picture name. Write the letter that stands for the first sound.

k j p n i

1

2

3

4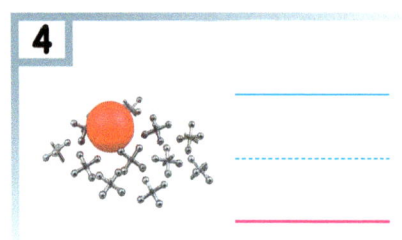

5

6

7

8

9

10

11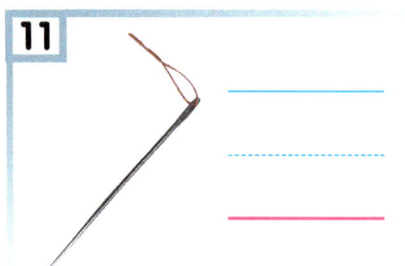

12

13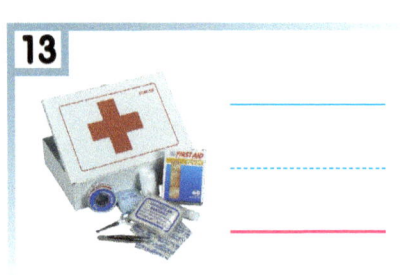

14

15

Unit 3: Assessing Initial *k, j, p, n, i*

Say the picture name. Fill in the circle next to the letter that stands for the last sound.

Unit 3 CHECK-UP

k p n

1. ○ k ● n ○ p (fan)
2. ○ n ● k ○ p (lake)
3. ○ p ○ n ● k (Canada map)
4. ○ n ○ p ● k (bike)
5. ● k ○ p ○ n (cup)
6. ● n ○ k ○ p (sun)
7. ● p ○ n ○ k (man — n)
8. ○ n ○ p ● k (rake)
9. ○ k ○ p ● n (jeep — p)
10. ● k ○ n ○ p (bird)
11. ○ n ○ k ● p (leaf)
12. ● p ○ n ○ k (snake)
13. ○ k ○ p ● n (train)
14. ● n ○ p ○ k (foam)
15. ○ k ● n ○ p (lion)

Unit 3: Assessing Final *k, p, n*

UNIT 4
Off We Go!

Consonants c, h, l, r, and Short Vowel u

JUST BECAUSE

Just ridin' my bike
With the wind in my hair....
Not really going....
....Anywhere

Not doing a thing
That I know I should....
Just ridin' my bike
Cause it feels so good.

Lois Simmie

Think About It

What other ways can people travel?
How do you like to travel?

Write l if the picture name begins with the l sound.

leaf

1

2

3

4

5

6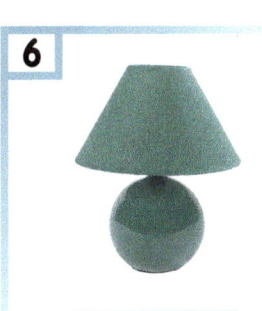

7

8

9

10

11

12

Say the name of each picture. Ask your child to lean to the left if the word begins with the l sound.

Unit 4: Initial Consonant *l*

Write r if the picture name begins with the r sound.

rake

1

2

3

4

5

6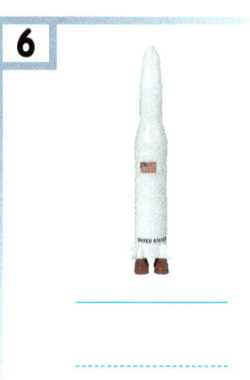

7

8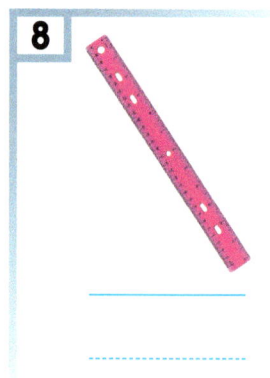

9

10

11

12

Unit 4: Initial Consonant *r*

Ask your child to name three objects in your home whose names begin with the **r** sound.

Say each picture name. Write the word in the correct box to name each picture.

Across →

1. [can]
2. [hit]
3. [cot]

Down ↓

4. [hat]
5. [rip]
6. [log]

Word bank: can, cot, hat, hit, log, rip

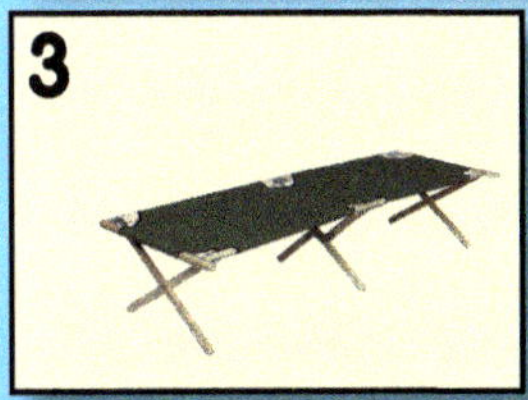

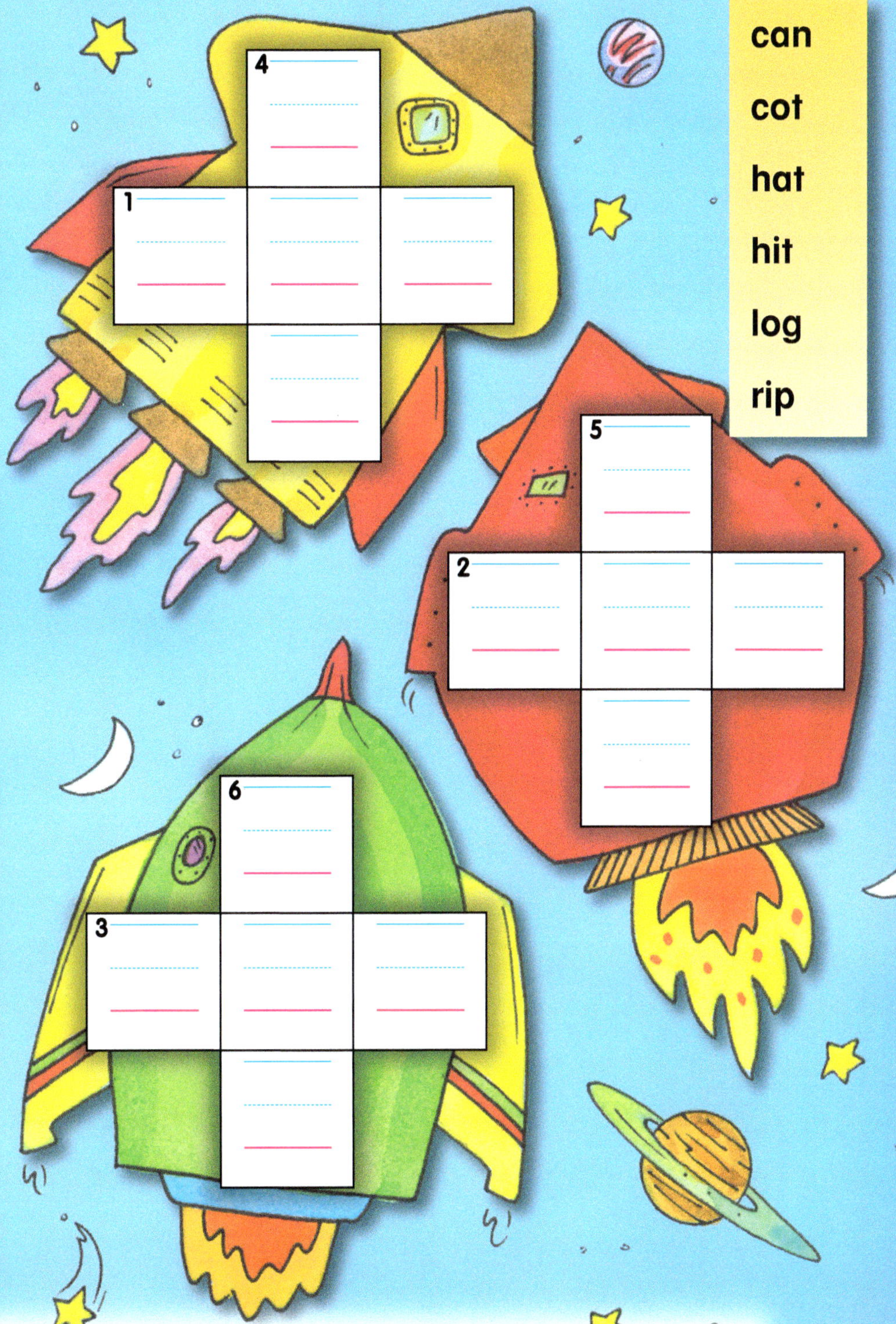

Unit 4: Initial *c, h, l, r* Review

Say the name of each picture. Write the letter that stands for the **first** sound in each picture name.

c　　h　　l　　r

1.
2.
3.
4.
5.
6.
7.
8.
9.
10.
11.
12.

Unit 4: Initial *c*, *h*, *l*, *r* Review

Ask your child to name two pictures whose names begin with each sound.

Name the pictures. Colour each picture whose name rhymes with the word part at the beginning of the row.

Say the word part. Then say the name of each picture. Circle and write the word.

-ug

1. rug   tug
2. mug   bug
3. jug   hug

-ut

4. but   nut
5. cut   rut
6. hut   cut

-ub

7. tub   cub
8. rub   sub
9. tub   hub

Unit 4: Short Vowel *u* Phonograms

AT HOME Help your child think of sentences using two of the rhyming words in each row.

Say the picture name. Write the letter that stands for the **first** sound.

c h l r u

1

2

3

4

5

6

7

8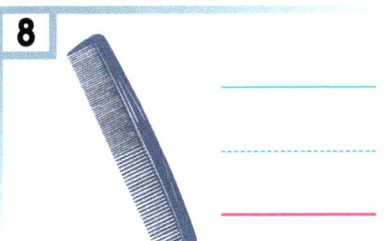

9

10

11

12

13

14

15

Unit 4: Assessing Initial *c, h, l, r, u*

71

Unit 4 CHECK-UP

Say the picture name. Fill in the circle next to the letter that stands for the vowel sound.

a o i u

1
- ○ a
- ○ i
- ○ o

2
- ○ o
- ○ u
- ○ i

3
- ○ i
- ○ u
- ○ a

4
- ○ u
- ○ a
- ○ o

5
- ○ o
- ○ i
- ○ a

6
- ○ i
- ○ u
- ○ o

7
- ○ o
- ○ u
- ○ i

8
- ○ o
- ○ a
- ○ u

9
- ○ u
- ○ a
- ○ i

10
- ○ a
- ○ o
- ○ i

11
- ○ o
- ○ u
- ○ a

12
- ○ i
- ○ u
- ○ o

13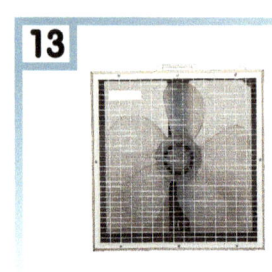
- ○ a
- ○ u
- ○ i

14
- ○ u
- ○ i
- ○ o

15
- ○ o
- ○ u
- ○ a

Unit 4: Assessing Short Vowels *a, o, i, u*

UNIT 5
At the Store

Consonants v, y, z, qu, x, and Short Vowel e

General Store

Some day I'm going
To have a store
With a tinkly bell
Hung over the door,
With real glass cases
And counters wide
And drawers all spilly
With things inside.
There'll be a little
Of everything:
Bolts of calico;
Balls of string;
Jars of peppermint;
Tins of tea;
Pots and kettles
And crockery;

It will be my store,
And I will say:
"What can I do
For you today?"

Rachel Field

Think About It

What kind of store would you like to have?
What would you say to your customers?

73

Write **v** if the picture name begins with the **v** sound.

vest

1 	2 	3 	4 
5 	6 	7 	8 
9 	10 	11 	12 

74 Unit 5: Initial Consonant **v**

Ask your child to complete the following sentence with a picture name that begins with the **v** sound: Val got a very big ___.

Extra Eggs

Excuse me, Emma.
Are the eggs all gone?
Are there any extras?
I like eggs at dawn.

Extra and **egg** have the short **e** sound. Circle each picture whose name has the short **e** sound.

Unit 5: Initial Short Vowel *e*

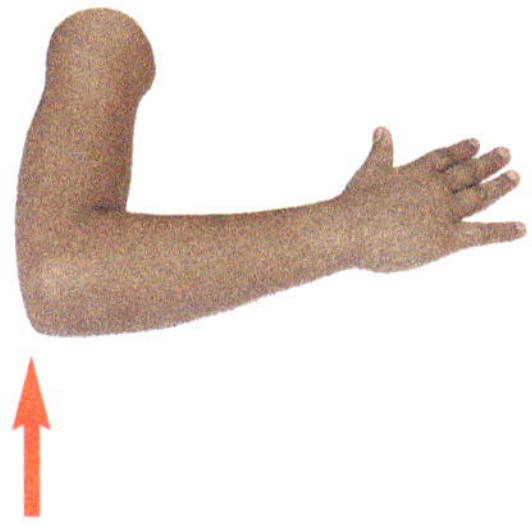

Name the pictures. Colour each picture whose name rhymes with the word part at the beginning of the row.

Unit 5: Short Vowel *e* Phonograms

Say the word part. Then say the name of each picture. Circle and write the word.

-ed

1. wed   red
2. led   bed
3. wed   fed

-et

4. let   jet
5. pet   yet
6. met   wet

-en

7. ten   men
8. den   pen
9. ten   hen

Help your child think of two more words that rhyme with the words in each row.

Say each picture name. Write the word in the puzzle that names each picture.

Across →

1. (balloon/top)
2. (log)
3. (gum)

Down ↓

4. (yell)
5. (mix)
6. (vet)
7. (axe)
8. (nap)

axe gum log mix nap top vet yell

Unit 5: Short Vowels *a, o, i, u, e* Review

85

Write e if you hear the short e sound in each picture name. Colour the pictures with the short e sound.

PHONICS and SPELLING

1. j e t
2. h e n
3. c _ p
4. t e n
5. n e t
6. b e d
7. p e n
8. k e g
9. b _ x

Unit 5: Spelling Short *e* Words

Look at the picture and read the sentence. Circle the word that completes the sentence. Write the word on the line.

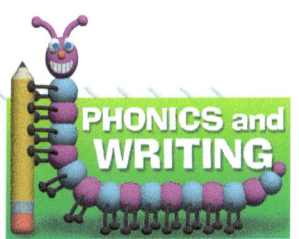

1. Zack went to _____ yellow socks.
   set   met   get

2. He got a _____ cap.
   bed   red   fed

3. Then he got a red _____.
   vest   nest   rest

4. Zack got red pants _____.
   text   next   rest

5. Zack did not get socks _____.
   yet   let   met

6. Quick, don't _____ Zack forget!
   bet   met   let

Take turns reading the sentences with your child. Ask your child to help you make a list of things to buy at a store.

Unit 5: Reading **v, y, z, qu, x** and Short Vowel **e** in Context

87

Write what you would buy from Meg and Ken's sale. Tell why. The words in the box may help you.

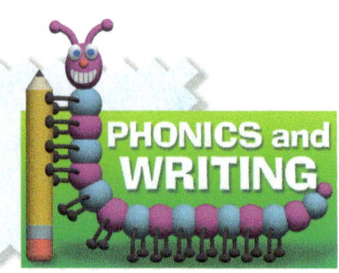

bed
bell
get
jet
net
pen
ten

Say the picture name. Write the letter or letters that stand for the first sound.

Unit 5 CHECK-UP

v y z qu e

1. 
2. 
3. 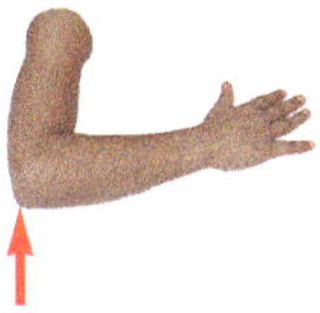
4. 
5. 
6. 
7. 
8. 
9. 
10. 
11. 
12. 
13. 
14. 
15.

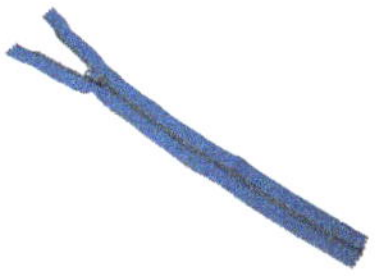

Unit 5: Assessing Initial *v, y, z, qu, e*

Unit 5 CHECK-UP

Say the picture name. Fill in the circle next to the letter that stands for the vowel sound.

a e i o u

1
○ a
○ e
○ u

2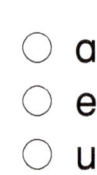
○ i
○ o
○ u

3
○ e
○ i
○ o

4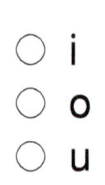
○ u
○ o
○ e

5
○ o
○ u
○ a

6
○ a
○ e
○ o

7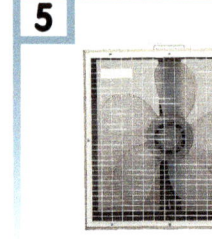
○ o
○ i
○ a

8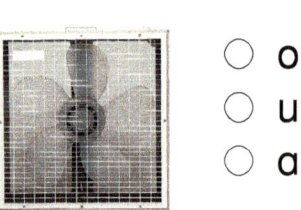
○ a
○ i
○ o

9
○ u
○ o
○ e

10
○ u
○ e
○ o

11
○ o
○ u
○ e

12
○ a
○ e
○ i

13
○ e
○ i
○ o

14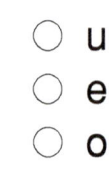
○ u
○ e
○ o

15
○ a
○ i
○ e

Unit 5: Assessing Short Vowels *a, e, i, o, u*

UNIT 6
Adventures
Long Vowels

Fishing

Waiting for a bite
By a cool stream
Is my very
Favourite dream.

On new, green grass
I sit and wait
Till the big one
Takes the bait.

How eagerly
I cast my line.
I feel the tug
And know the sign.

I reel it in
How fine it looks!
Should I throw it back
To its shady brook?

Sheree Haughian

Think About It

How would you catch a fish?
What adventures have you had?

Say each picture name. Write a–e if the picture name has the long a sound.

r a k e

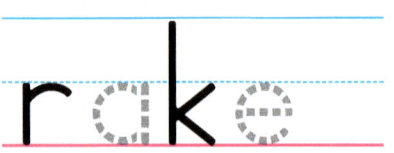
rake

1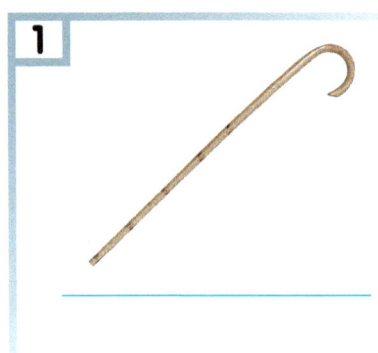
c a n e

2
c _ p

3
c _ p

4
g _ t

5
m _ n

6
t _ p

7
s _ f

8
c _ k

9
l _ k

Say each picture name. Ask your child to wave if the picture name has the long a sound.

Unit 6: Long Vowel a

Sail on the Bay

Ray will sail
Today with Gail.
Rain, stay away
On the bay!

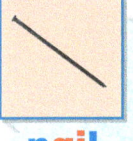 
nail hay

Nail and **hay** have the long **a** sound. The letters **ai** and **ay** can stand for the long **a** sound. Say each picture name and circle it. Write the name.

1.  way / (wait) — w a i t
2.  pay / pain — p
3.  sail / say — s l
4.  rail / ray — r
5.  may / mail — m l
6.  jay / jail — j
7.  pail / pay — p l
8.  tail / hay — t l
9.  rain / ray — r n

Unit 6: Long Vowel *a*

Name the pictures. Colour each picture whose name rhymes with the word part at the beginning of the row.

1. -ail

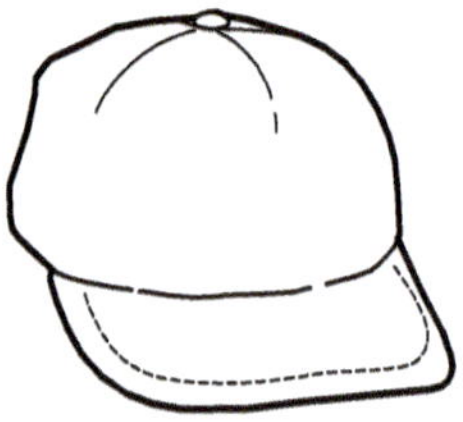

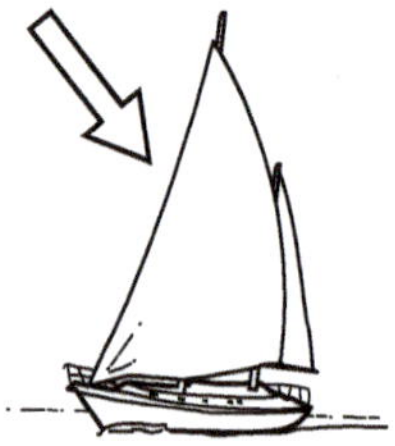

2. -ake

3. -ay

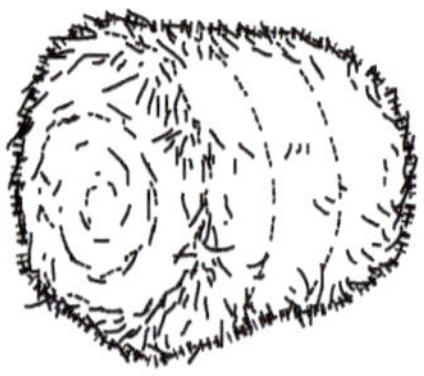

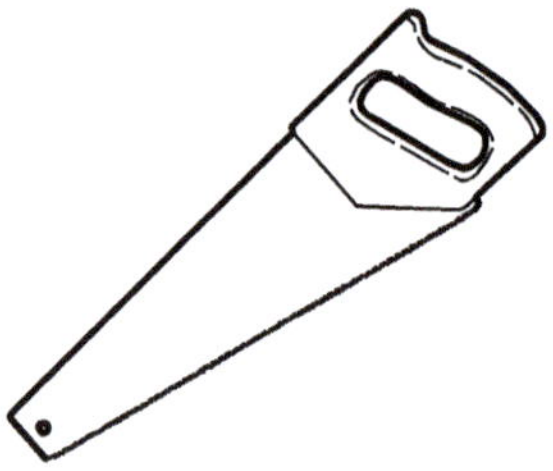

4. -ane

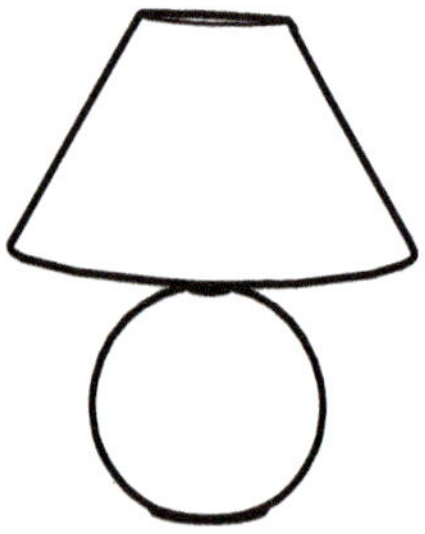

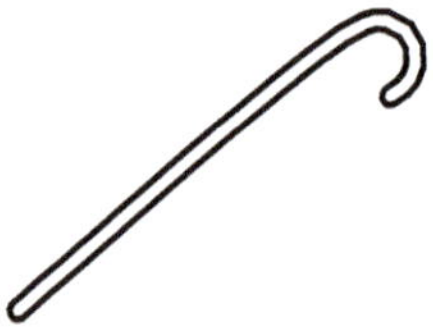

5. -ain

Unit 6: Long Vowel *a* Phonograms

Look at the picture and read the sentence. Circle the word that completes the sentence. Write the word on the line.

1. Kate wants to _____ .
   way   play   pat

2. It is a rainy _____ .
   day   may   dad

3. Kate gets her _____ hat.
   ran   main   rain

4. She will _____ her umbrella.
   take   tap   lake

5. One puddle is as big as a _____ .
   lap   bake   lake

6. Kate _____ play in the rain all day.
   say   may   mat

Unit 6: Reading Long *a* in Context

What game can you play on a rainy day? Write about it. The words in the box may help you.

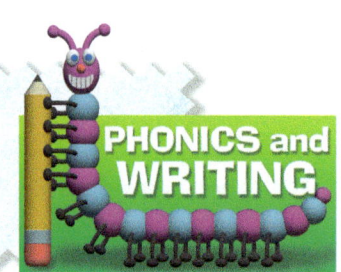

game
make
pay
play
tape
wait

Unit 6: Writing Long *a* Words

Ask your child to read the story to you.

Say each picture name. Write o–e if the picture name has the long o sound.

bone

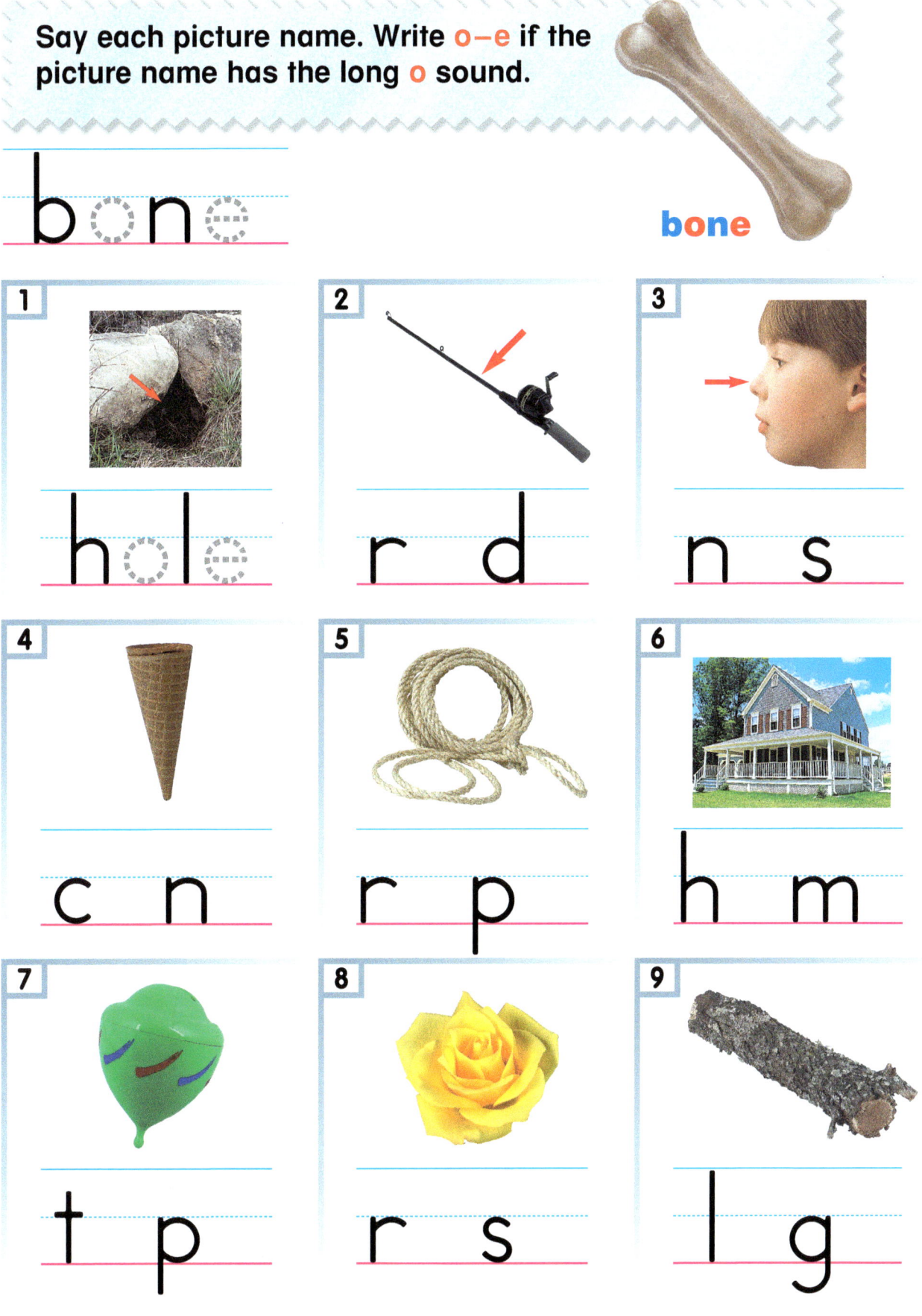

1. hole
2. r d
3. n s
4. c n
5. r p
6. h m
7. t p
8. r s
9. l g

Ask your child to name all the pictures whose names have the long o sound.

Unit 6: Long Vowel o 97

The letters o–e and oa can stand for the long o sound.
Say each picture name and circle it. Write the name.

bone

coat

1. not / (note) — note
2. goat / got — g___t
3. hot / hole — h___l
4. rob / robe — r___b
5. coat / cot — c___t
6. rod / road — r___d
7. home / hop — h___m
8. sob / soap — s___p
9. cob / cone — c___n

98 Unit 6: Long Vowel o

Point to some of the words your child wrote and ask him or her to read them.

Name the pictures. Colour each picture whose name rhymes with the word part at the beginning of the row.

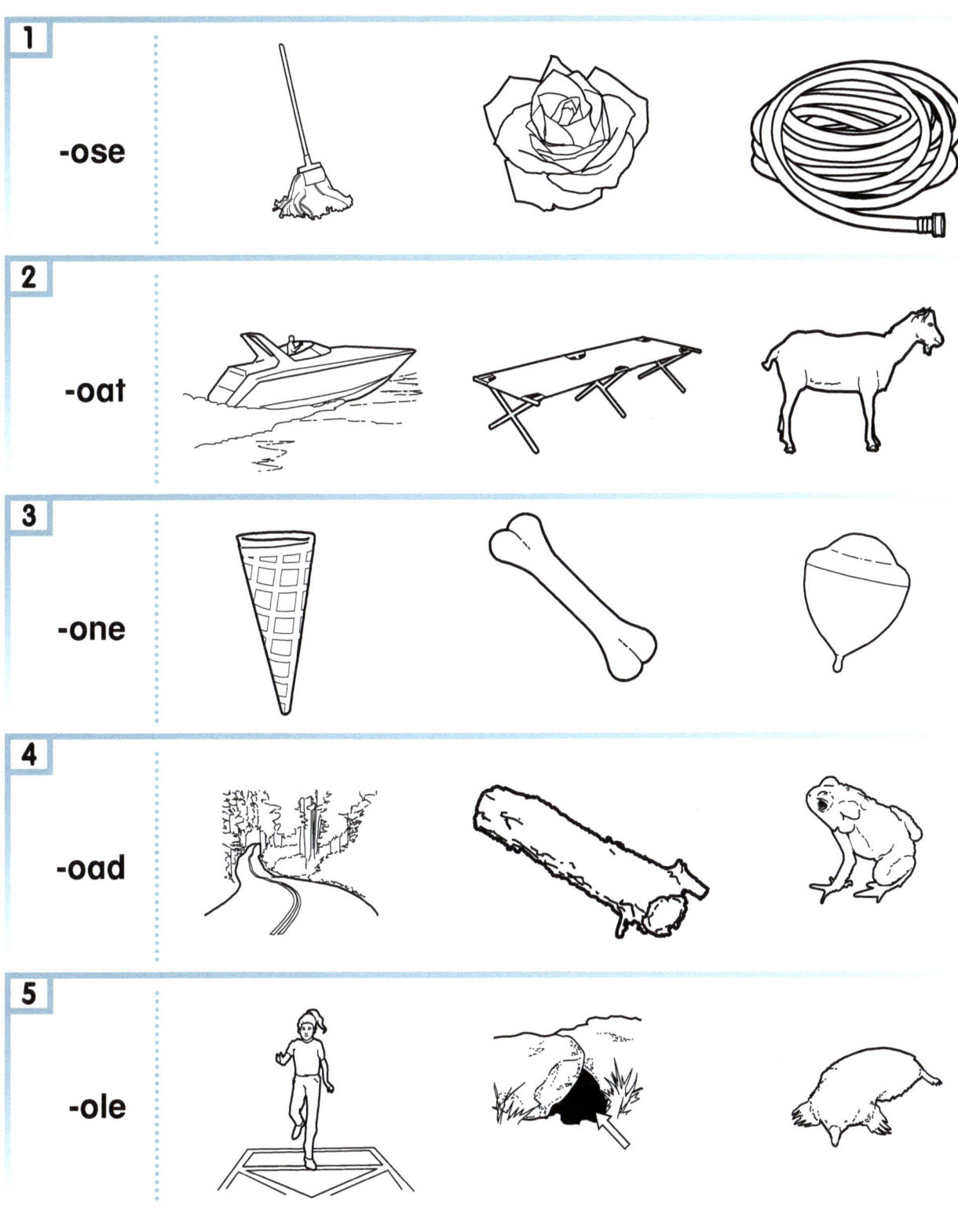

Unit 6: Long Vowel *o* Phonograms

Say the word part. Then say the name of each picture. Circle and write the word.

-oat

1. boat   coat
2. float   goat
3. coat   boat

-ose

4. rose   nose
5. pose   hose
6. rose   hose

-ole

7. role   mole
8. hole   mole
9. pole   role

Say each picture name. Write the word from the box if you hear the long o sound. In the last box, draw a long o picture. Write the name.

PHONICS and SPELLING

| boat | bone | coat | cot | not | note |
| road | rob | robe | rod | soap | toad |

1. soap
2. cot
3. note
4. robe
5. toad
6. boat
7. rod
8. bone
9.

Unit 6: Spelling Long *o* Words 101

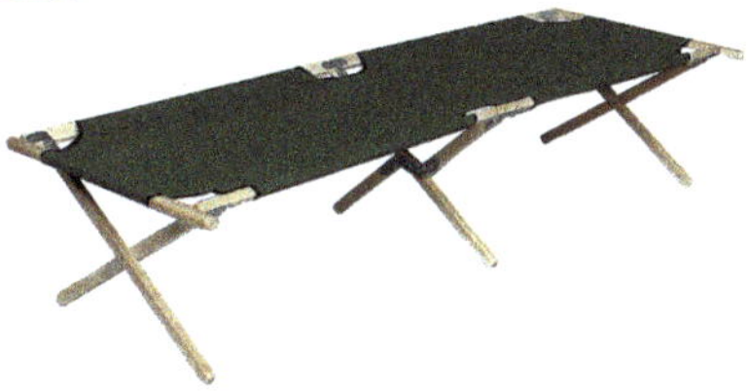

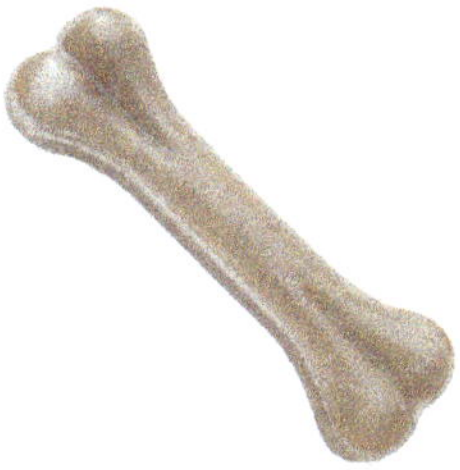

Look at the picture and read the sentence. Circle the word that completes the sentence. Write the word on the line.

PHONICS and READING

1.  Ben's pal Joe went to a new _____ .

   bone   home   hop

2.  Ben will miss _____ .

   Toe   Bob   Joe

3.  Ben got a _____ from Joe in the mail.

   note   vote   not

4.  Joe's home is on a _____ to a lake.

   rod   load   road

5. Ben can go on a _____ with Joe.

   boat   pot   coat

6.  The boys will have fun at the _____ .

   log   bake   lake

Unit 6: Reading Long *o* in Context

AT HOME Take turns reading the sentences with your child.

What do you think Joe the mole will do at the lake? Write about it. The words in the box may help you.

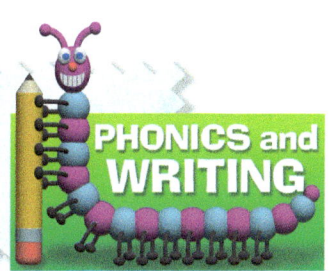

boat
coat
home
mole
pole
woke

Ask your child to read the story to you.
Have your child point out the long o words.

Unit 6: Writing Long *o* Words

Say each picture name. Write i–e if the picture name has the long i sound.

k i t e

kite

1	2	3	4
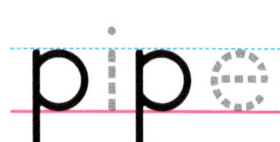		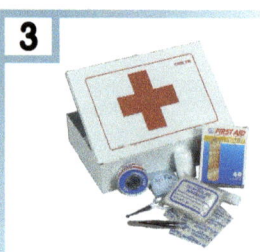	
p i p e	t r	k t	b k
5	6	7	8
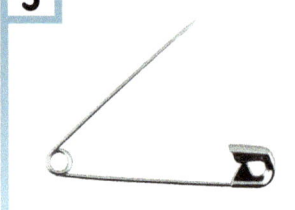			
p n	h d	v n	d m
9	10	11	12

n n	r p	m k	d v

104 Unit 6: Long Vowel *i*

Ask your child to name all the pictures whose names have the long **i** sound.

Name the pictures. Colour each picture whose name rhymes with the word part at the beginning of the row.

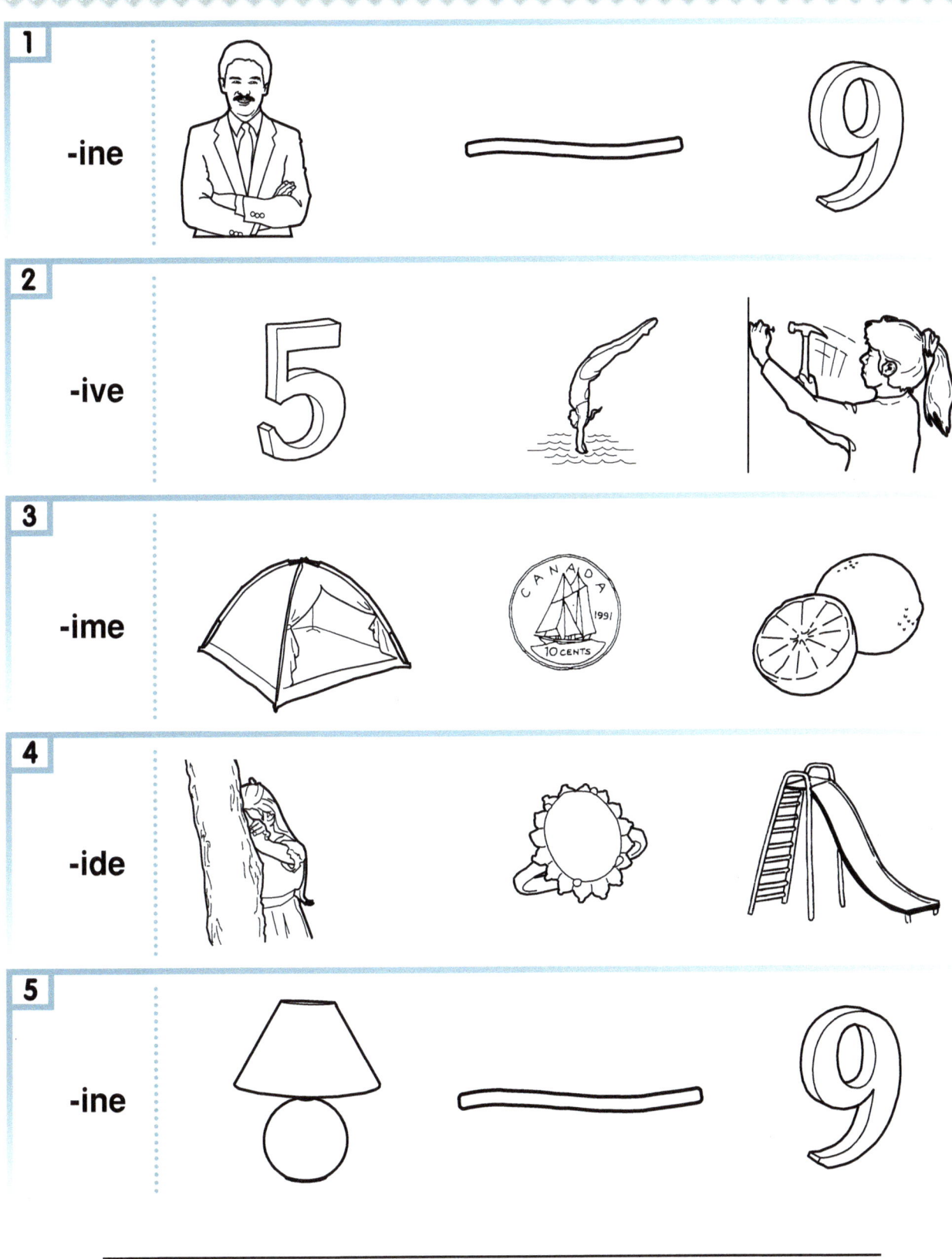

Say the word part. Then say the name of each picture. Circle and write the word.

-ike

1. like   hike
2. bike   hike
3. mike   like

-ice

4. dice   nice
5. rice   mice
6. nice   rice

-ine

7. fine   vine
8. dine   pine
9. nine   line

Say each picture name. Write the word from the box if you hear the long i sound. In the last box, draw a long i picture. Write the name.

PHONICS and SPELLING

| bike | bite | fin | fine | five | kit |
| kite | mice | mine | nine | pin | pine |

1. nine
2.
3. mice
4. bike
5.
6. kite
7. pine
8. five
9.

Unit 6: Spelling Long *i* Words

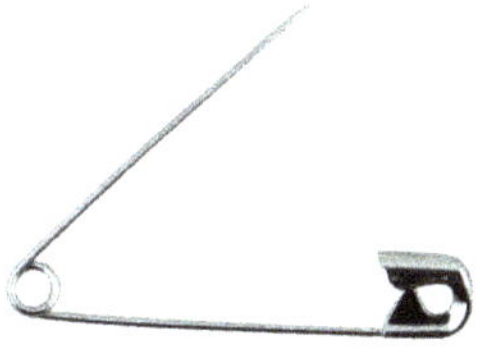

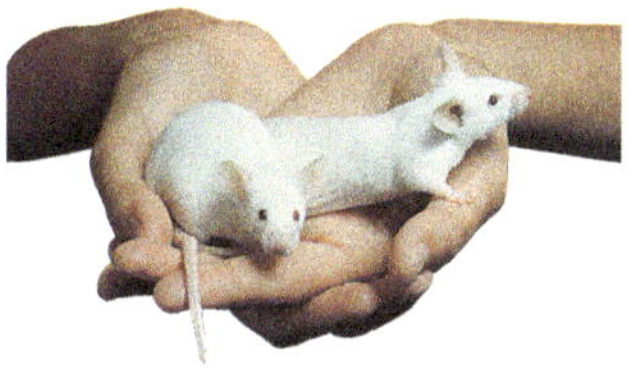

Look at the picture and read the sentence. Circle the word that completes the sentence. Write the word on the line.

1.  Five _____ have a fine home.
   mix   rice   mice

2.  The five mice _____ bikes.
   ride   hide   rip

3.  They _____ to slide.
   lit   like   mike

4. The mice see a _____ snack.
   mine   fin   fine

5.  Oh no, the cat sees the _____ mice!
   nine   five   fix

6.  The five mice _____.
   hide   ride   hit

108 Unit 6: Reading Long *i* in Context

Ask your child to read a sentence and name all the words that have the long *i* sound.

Do you like to ride a bike or hike? Write about it. The words in the box may help you.

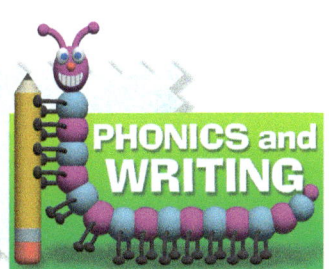

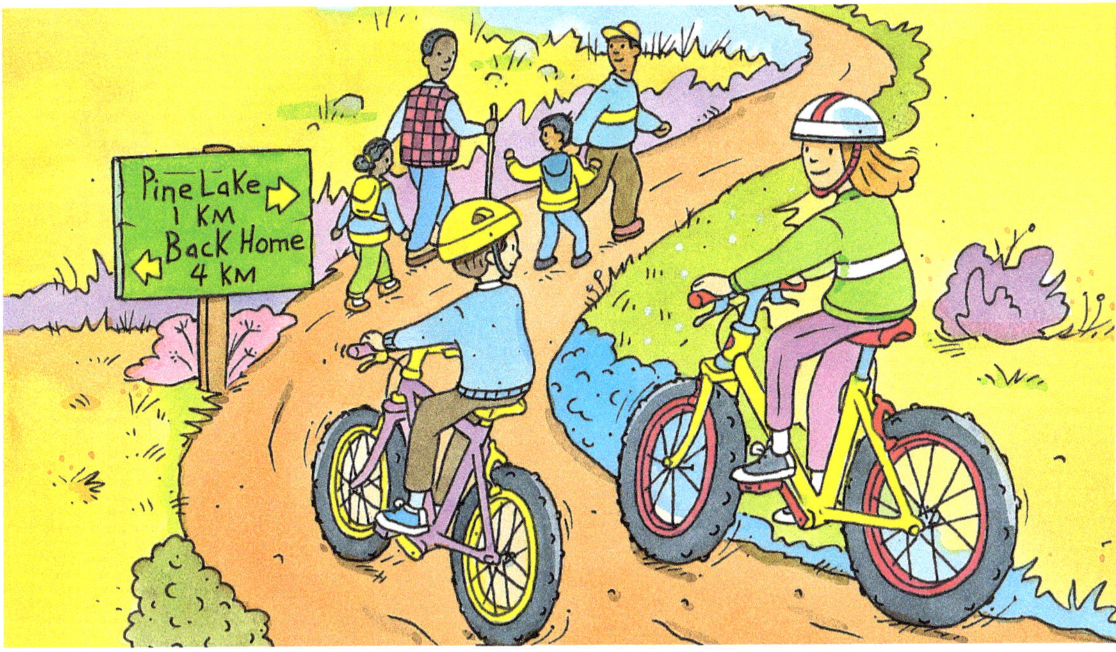

bike
five
like
tire
mine
ride

Say each picture name. Write u–e if the picture name has the long u sound.

c u b e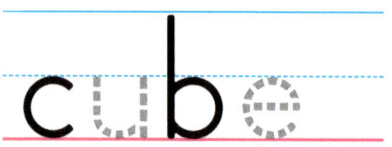
cube

1. 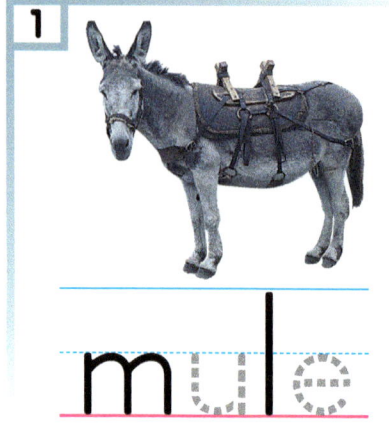 m u l e
2.  c _ t
3.  J _ n
4. 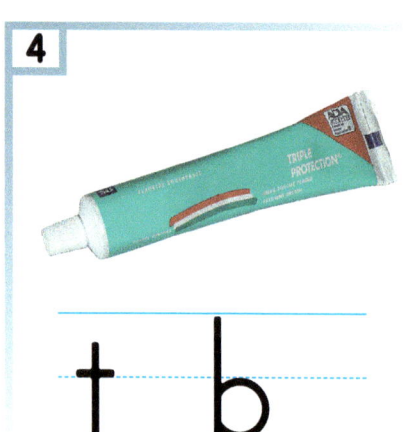 t _ b
5.  _ s _
6.  b _ s
7.  d _ n
8.  j _ g
9. 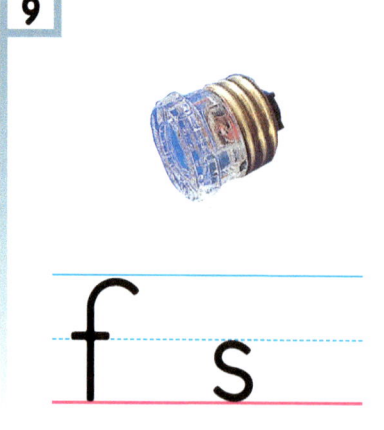 f _ s

**Circle the word that names the picture.
Write the word.**

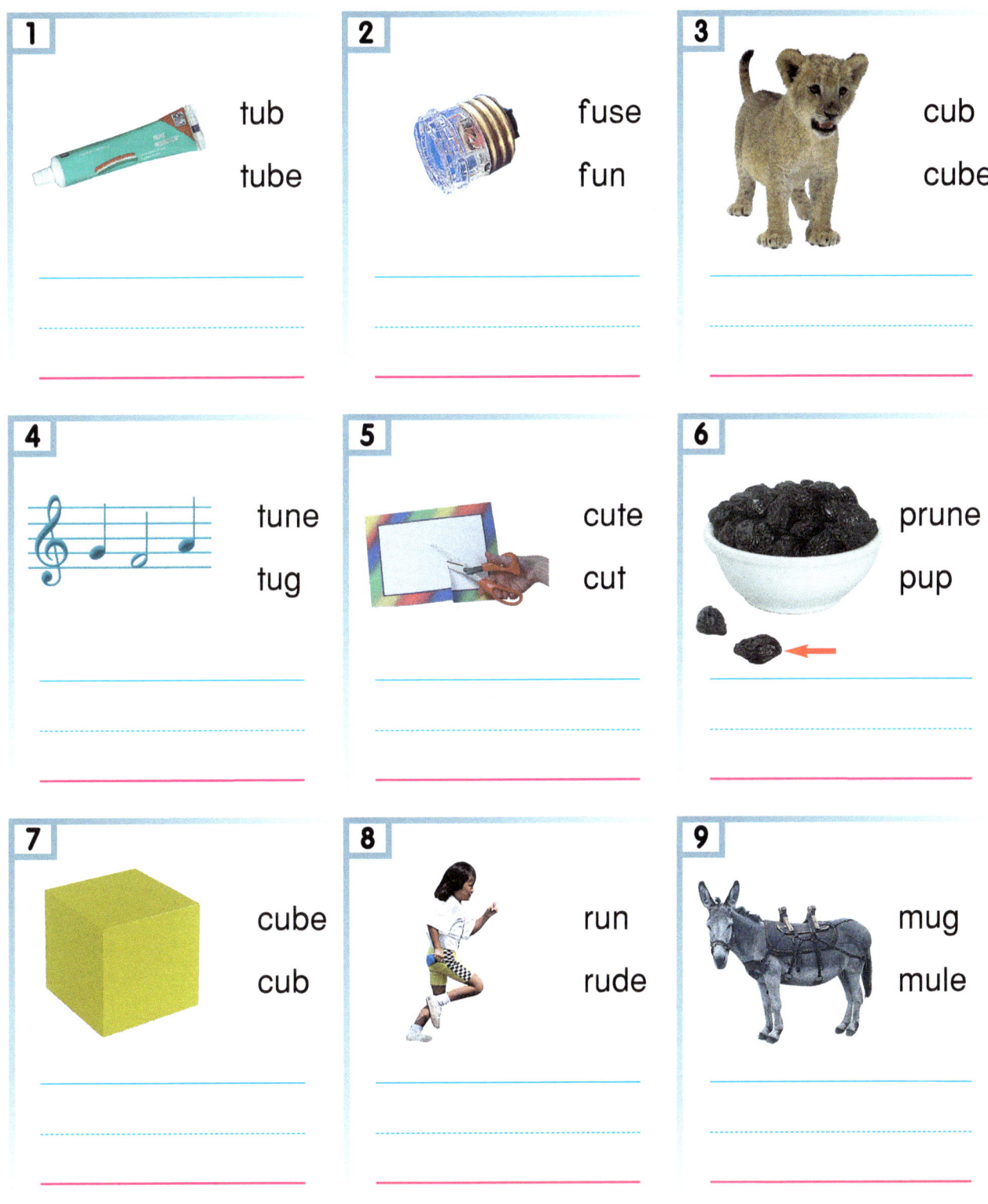

Unit 6: Long Vowel *u*

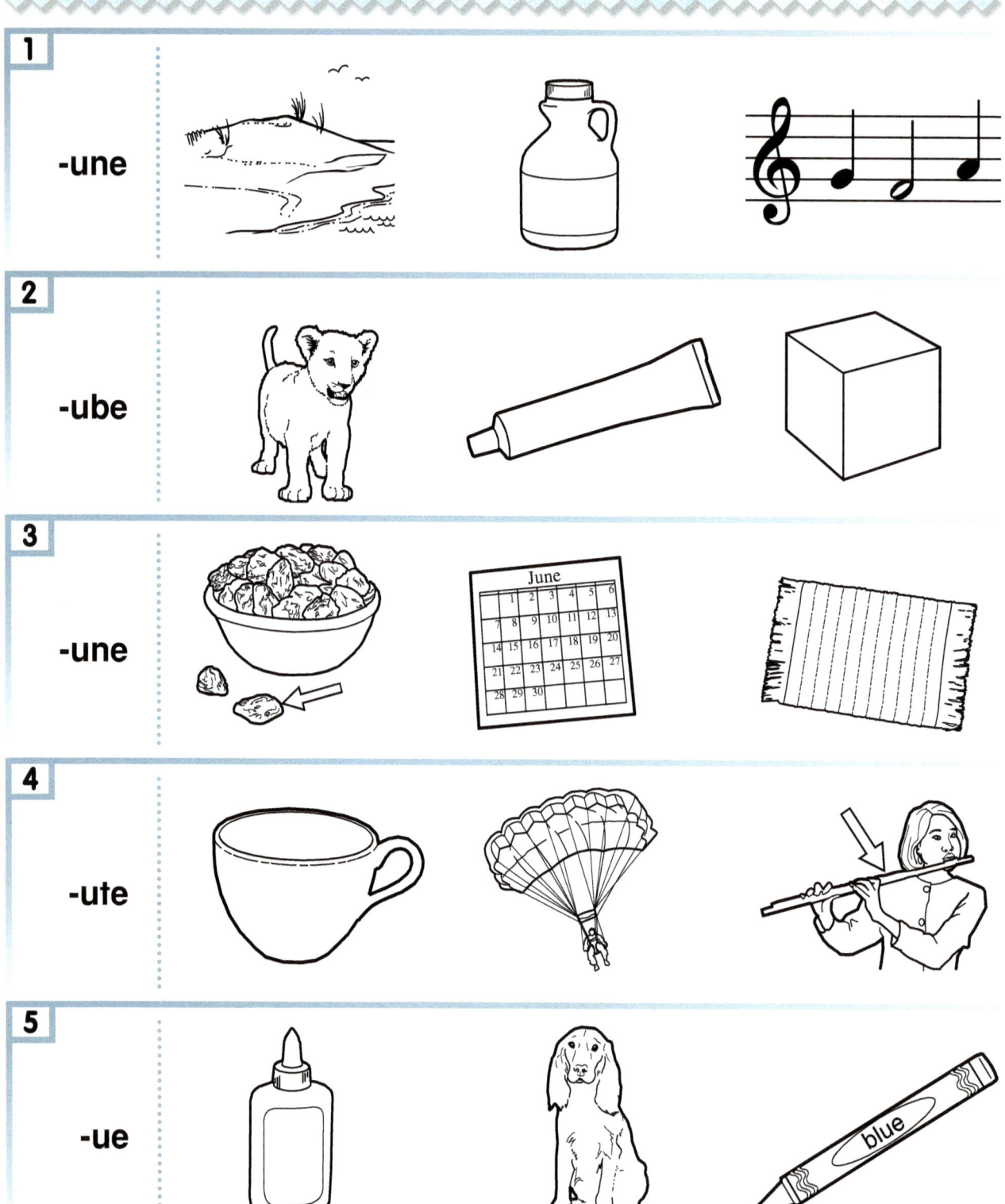

Say the word part. Then say the name of each picture. Circle and write the word.

-une

1. dune   June   tune

2. dune   tune   June

-ube

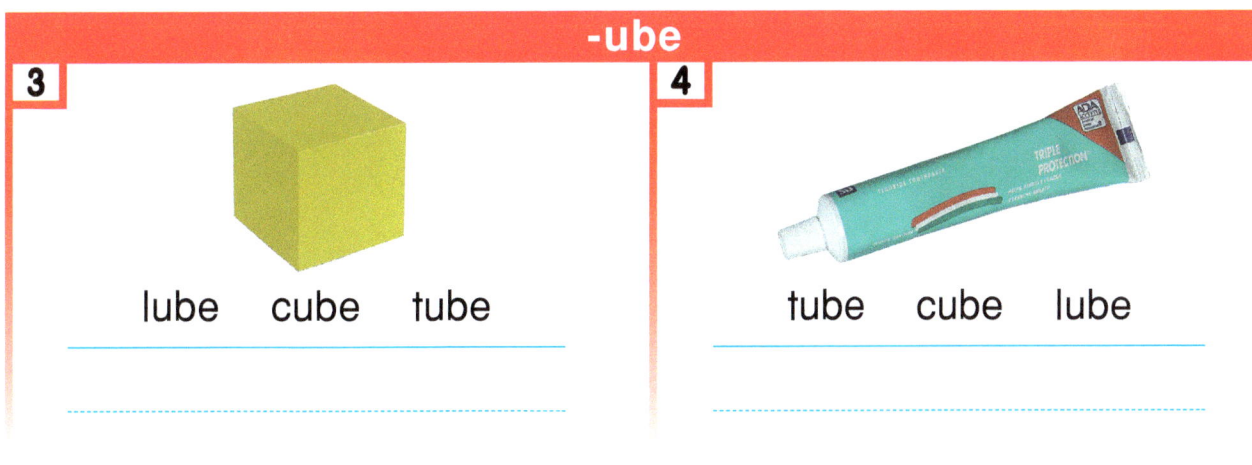

3. lube   cube   tube

4. tube   cube   lube

-une

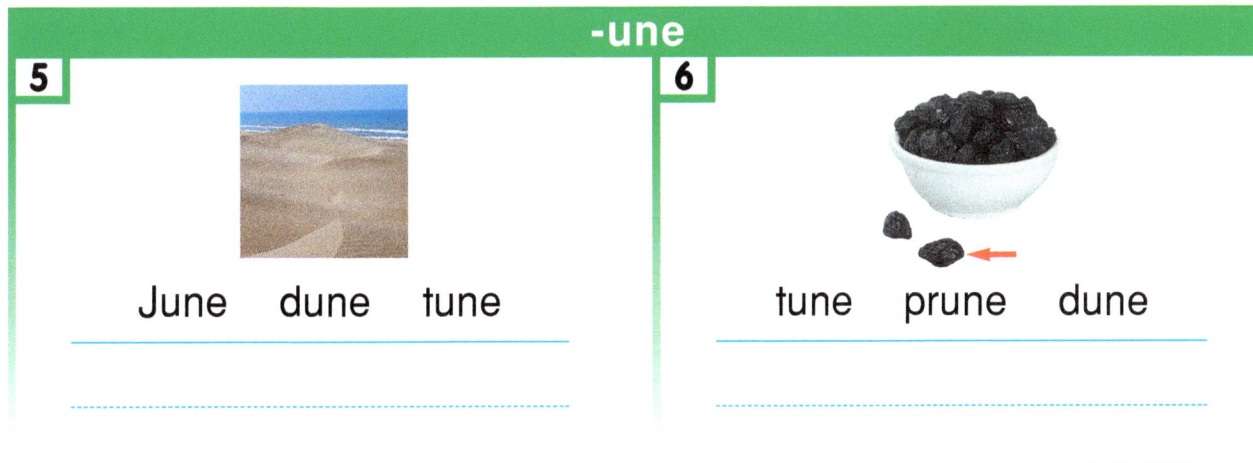

5. June   dune   tune

6. tune   prune   dune

Ask your child to use the circled words in sentences.

Unit 6: Long Vowel *u* Phonograms

Say each picture name. Write the word from the box if you hear the long u sound. In the last box, draw a long u picture. Write the name.

PHONICS and SPELLING

| cube | cut | cute | dune | flute | fuse |
| mug | mule | tub | tube | tug | tune |

1  tube

2 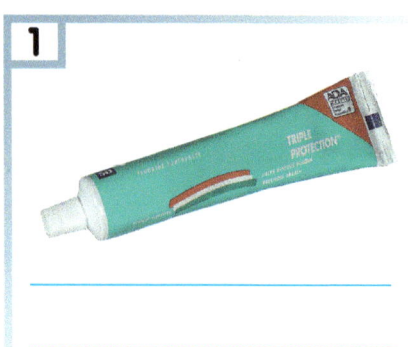 dune

3

4 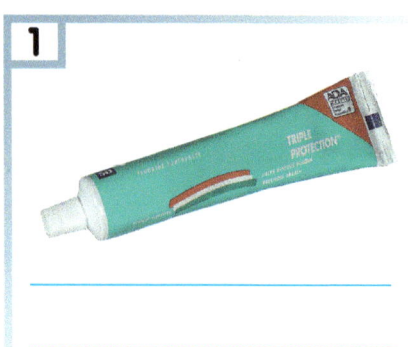 mule

5  tune

6  fuse

7

8  cube

9

Unit 6: Spelling Long *u* Words

Look at the picture and read the sentence. Circle the word that completes the sentence. Write the word on the line.

1. Bill can play the _____.
   fun   fuse   flute

2. A flute looks like a _____.
   tub   tube   cube

3. Bill plays a _____ in the woods.
   tune   June   nut

4. A _____ cub likes the tune.
   cut   cute   tube

5. The cub's mom is _____.
   huge   hug   hut

6. Mom led her _____ home.
   cube   cute   cub

Ask your child to point to and read ten words that have the long **u** sound.

Unit 6: Reading Long *u* in Context

115

Where would you ride if you had a mule? Write about it. The words in the box may help you.

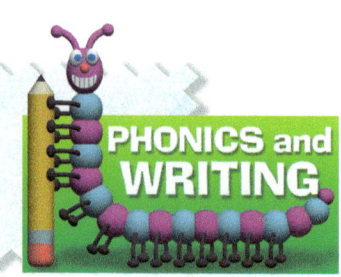

| cube |
| cute |
| dune |
| huge |
| mule |
| use |

Say each picture name. Write the missing letters and trace the vowels.

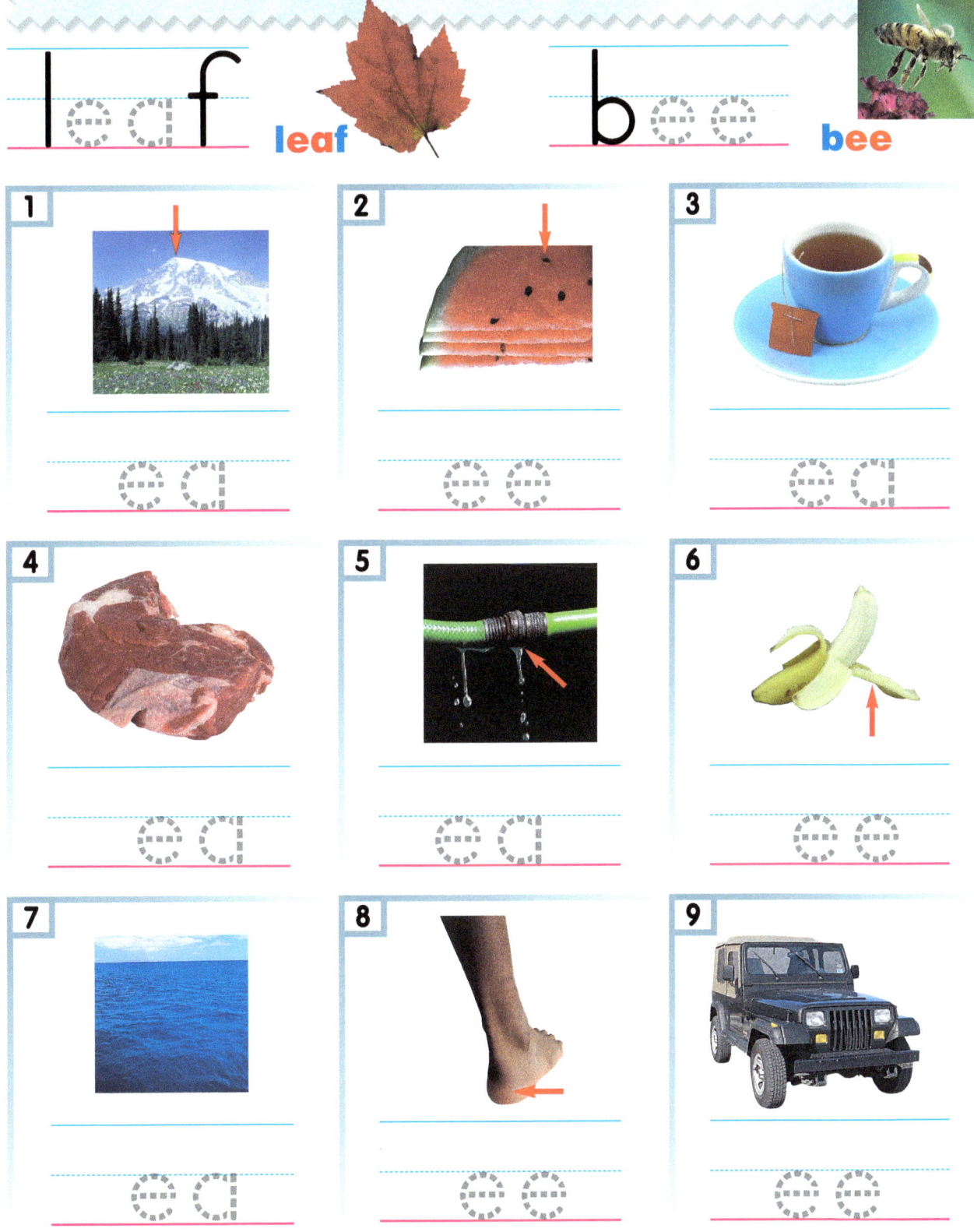

Ask your child to complete this sentence with a long e word: Lee sees a ____.

Unit 6: Long Vowel *e*

**Circle the word that names the picture.
Write the word.**

1
red
road
read

2
pet
peek
pine

3
meet
meal
mat

4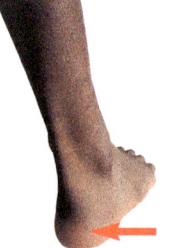
heat
heel
hen

5
sail
sat
seal

6
bee
tea
bean

7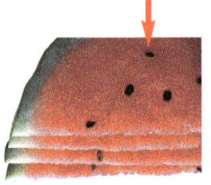
see
seed
seat

8
tame
team
ten

9
sea
seed
seat

Name the pictures. Colour each picture whose name rhymes with the word part at the beginning of the row.

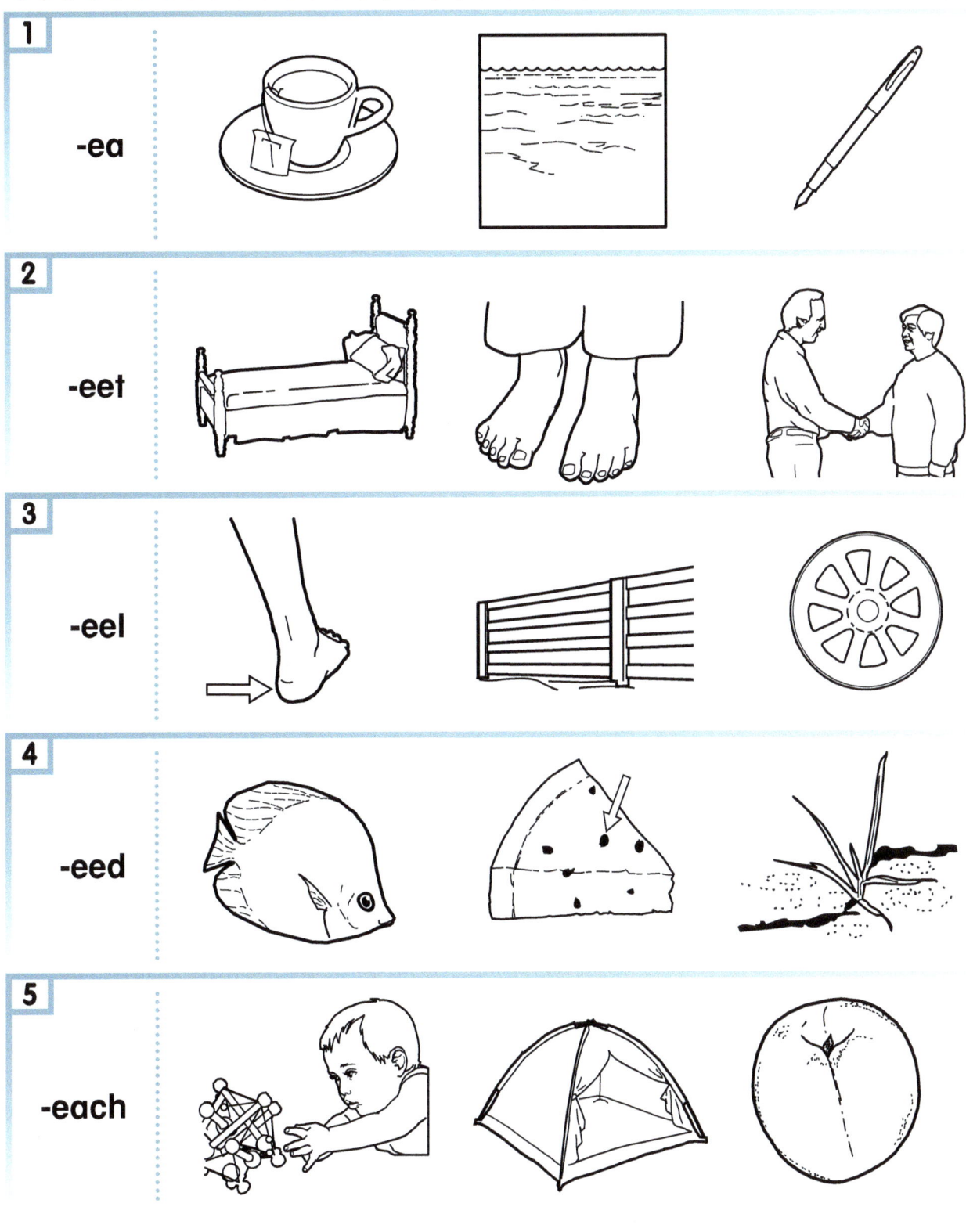

1. -ea
2. -eet
3. -eel
4. -eed
5. -each

Unit 6: Long Vowel *e* Phonograms

Say the word part. Then say the name of each picture. Circle and write the word.

-eak

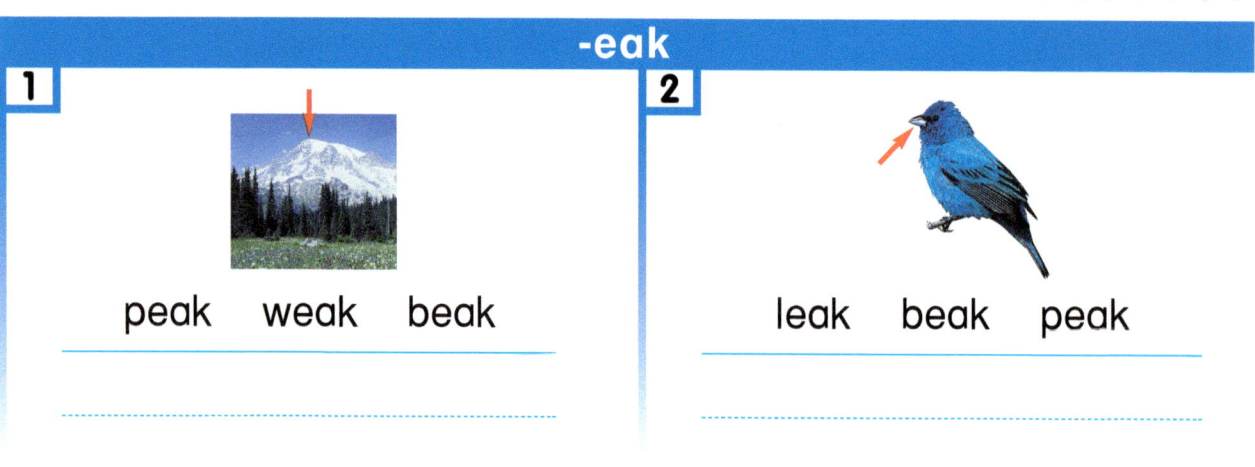

1. peak   weak   beak

2. leak   beak   peak

-eel

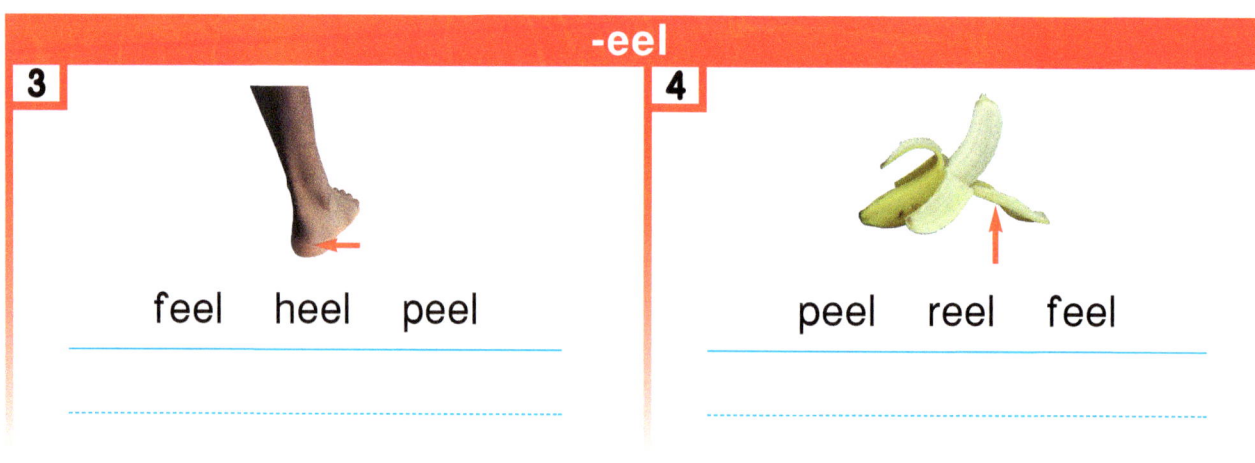

3. feel   heel   peel

4. peel   reel   feel

-eat

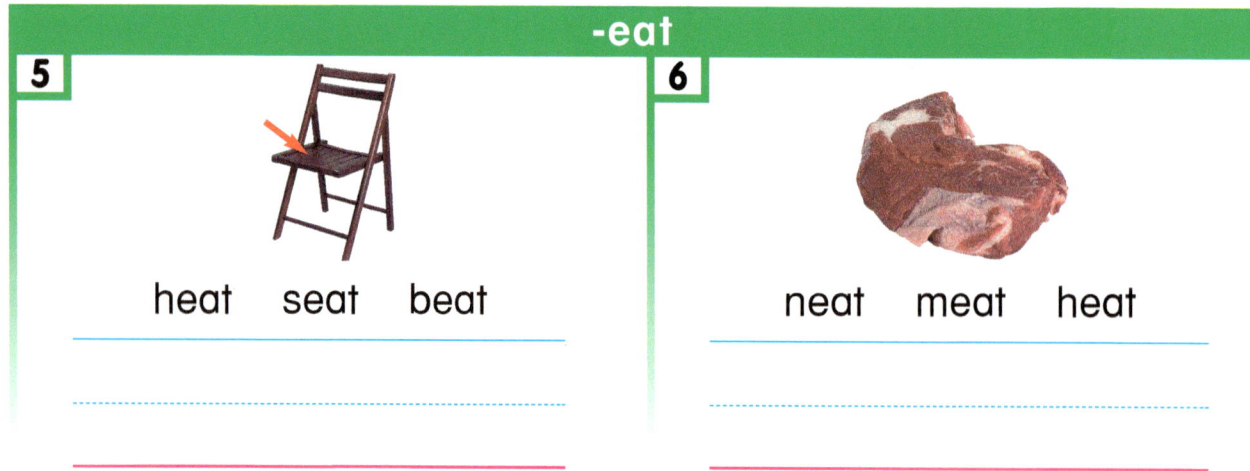

5. heat   seat   beat

6. neat   meat   heat

Say a picture name. Ask your child to say a word that rhymes.

Say each picture name. Write the word from the box if you hear the long e sound. In the last box, draw a long e picture. Write the word.

PHONICS and SPELLING

| bead | bed | heel | meet | read | red |
| seal | seat | tea | ten | weed | wet |

1. seal
2. 
3. 
4. read
5. weed
6.
7. heel
8. tea
9.

Unit 6: Spelling Long *e* Words

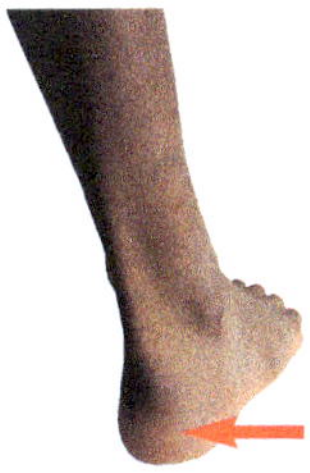

Look at the picture and read the sentence. Circle the word that completes the sentence. Write the word on the line.

1.  The octopus lives in the _____.

   set   seal   sea

2.  It has eight legs but no _____.

   feel   feet   fed

3.  Its mouth is like a _____.

   beak   bee   bell

4.  It likes to _____ clams.

   eel   eat   egg

5. It does not want to _____ you.

   meet   men   meal

6.  An octopus is really _____ to see.

   neat   net   beat

Unit 6: Reading Long *e* in Context

Ask your child to read the sentences. Ask what your child thinks is most interesting about an octopus.

What do you think Cub the bear will eat for his next meal? Write about it. The words in the box may help you.

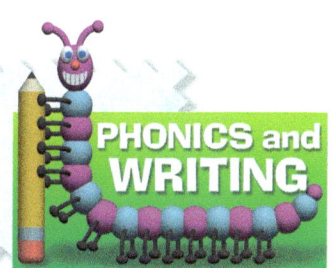

eat
tree
meal
meat
peel
see

Ask your child to read the story to you. Have your child find words in the picture that have a long vowel sound.

Unit 6: Writing Long *e* Words

Say each picture name. Write the word.

bab**y**  **baby**   fl**y**  **fly**

1. 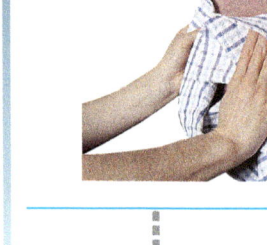 penny
2.  dry
3. 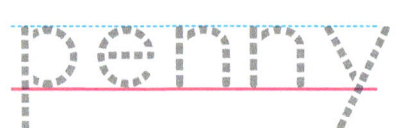 jell_
4. 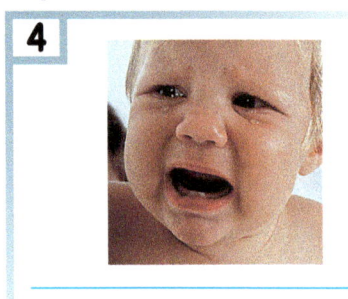 cr_
5.  bunn_
6.  lad_
7.  cit_
8.  sk_
9.  funn_

Unit 6: Final **y** as a Vowel

Have your child use some of the words on this page in sentences.

Say the picture name. Circle the picture name. Write the word.

Unit 6 CHECK-UP

1.  not / note

2.  pine / pin

3.  set / seat

4.  cape / cap

5.  weed / wed

6.  rod / road

7.  cup / cry

8.  ran / rain

9. cube / cub

Unit 6: Assessing Long Vowels 125

Unit 6 CHECK-UP

Say the picture name. Fill in the circle next to the picture name.

1
- ○ road
- ○ read
- ○ ride

2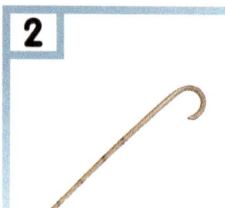
- ○ cane
- ○ coat
- ○ cone

3
- ○ lady
- ○ lake
- ○ load

4
- ○ ripe
- ○ road
- ○ rope

5
- ○ dry
- ○ day
- ○ dice

6
- ○ mile
- ○ mule
- ○ mail

7
- ○ bake
- ○ bike
- ○ beak

8
- ○ joke
- ○ jeep
- ○ jay

9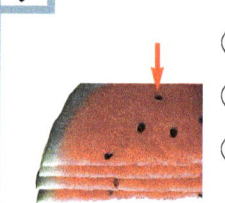
- ○ side
- ○ seed
- ○ sail

10
- ○ bait
- ○ beat
- ○ boat

11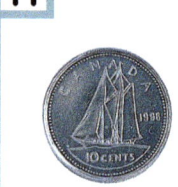
- ○ dome
- ○ dime
- ○ day

12
- ○ pail
- ○ peel
- ○ pile

13
- ○ meat
- ○ mane
- ○ mine

14
- ○ say
- ○ sea
- ○ sky

15
- ○ like
- ○ lake
- ○ leak

Unit 6: Assessing Long Vowels

UNIT 7
Make-Believe
Consonant Blends and Digraphs

Friends

I have a friend named Winchell,
My parents never see.
He's your imagination,
My parents say to me.

Me and Winchell, we don't mind,
We know it's all pretend.
What they don't know is,
Winchell's real,
I'm his
Imaginary friend.

Tim Wynne-Jones

Think About It

What pretend games do you play?
Why is it fun to pretend?

127

Circle the word that names the picture. Write the word.

1.
   soap
   stove
   snore

2.
   side
   smile
   slide

3.
   sky
   stay
   say

4.
   soak
   smoke
   stone

5.
   seat
   sled
   steps

6.
   snake
   sake
   skate

7.
   state
   skate
   sale

8.
   sail
   snail
   stain

9.
   skid
   sled
   seed

Unit 7: Initial Consonant Blends with *s*

Have your child say each picture name and spell the first two letters of the word.

**Circle the word that names the picture.
Write the word.**

1. sob / slot / spot

2. tip / twig / skip

3. scale / sale / snail

4. sing / sting / swing

5. soon / spoon / swoop

6. tens / spins / twins

7. scout / soak / spout

8. twin / sit / swim

9. sill / spill / skill

**Circle the word that names the picture.
Write the word.**

1

dine
drain
train

2
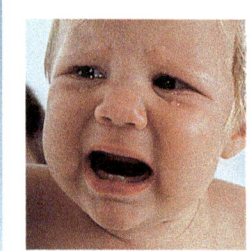
cry
cup
dry

3

bush
crush
brush

4

fog
frog
drop

5

back
drip
brick

6

dug
drum
brim

7

brag
cab
crab

8

bread
bike
drive

9

fires
fries
dries

**Circle the word that names the picture.
Write the word.**

1. tray / pray / fray

2. skill / drill / grill

3. dice / price / twice

4. dream / green / grain

5. bride / drive / prize

6. brain / rain / train

7. drapes / grapes / gates

8. tea / free / tree

9. grass / brass / press

**Circle the word that names the picture.
Write the word.**

1.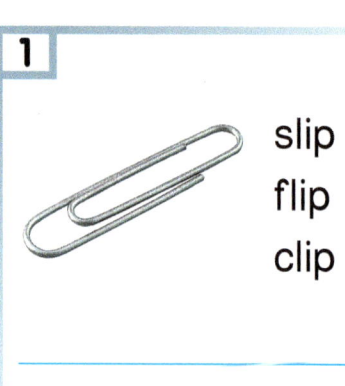
slip
flip
clip

2.
fuse
flute
brute

3.
flake
plate
grate

4.
gas
glass
grass

5.
bell
blue
glue

6.
coal
block
clock

7.
flag
brag
fall

8.
back
flock
block

9.
pant
plant
slant

Look at the picture and read the sentence. Circle the word that completes the sentence. Write the word on the line.

1. Flip was a _____ in a green pond.
   free   frog   flap

2. He _____ and hopped and ate flies.
   swam   swing   sweet

3. Flip wanted to _____ like a swan.
   flag   crab   fly

4. All _____ could do was hop.
   Flop   Flip   Drip

5. Flip did not _____.
   crisp   cry   creek

6. "I'll _____ in the water," he said.
   glad   grand   glide

Unit 7: Reading Consonant Blends in Context

The words in the box are hidden in the puzzle. Circle each word in the puzzle. Then write the word next to its picture.

```
r s k a t e z
p l u g w r l
l i d r e s s
s p i l l t w
f l a g v a a
f r a m e r n
```

dress   slip
flag   spill
frame   star
plug   swan
skate   twelve

1.
2.
3.
4.
5.
6.
7.
8.
9.
10.

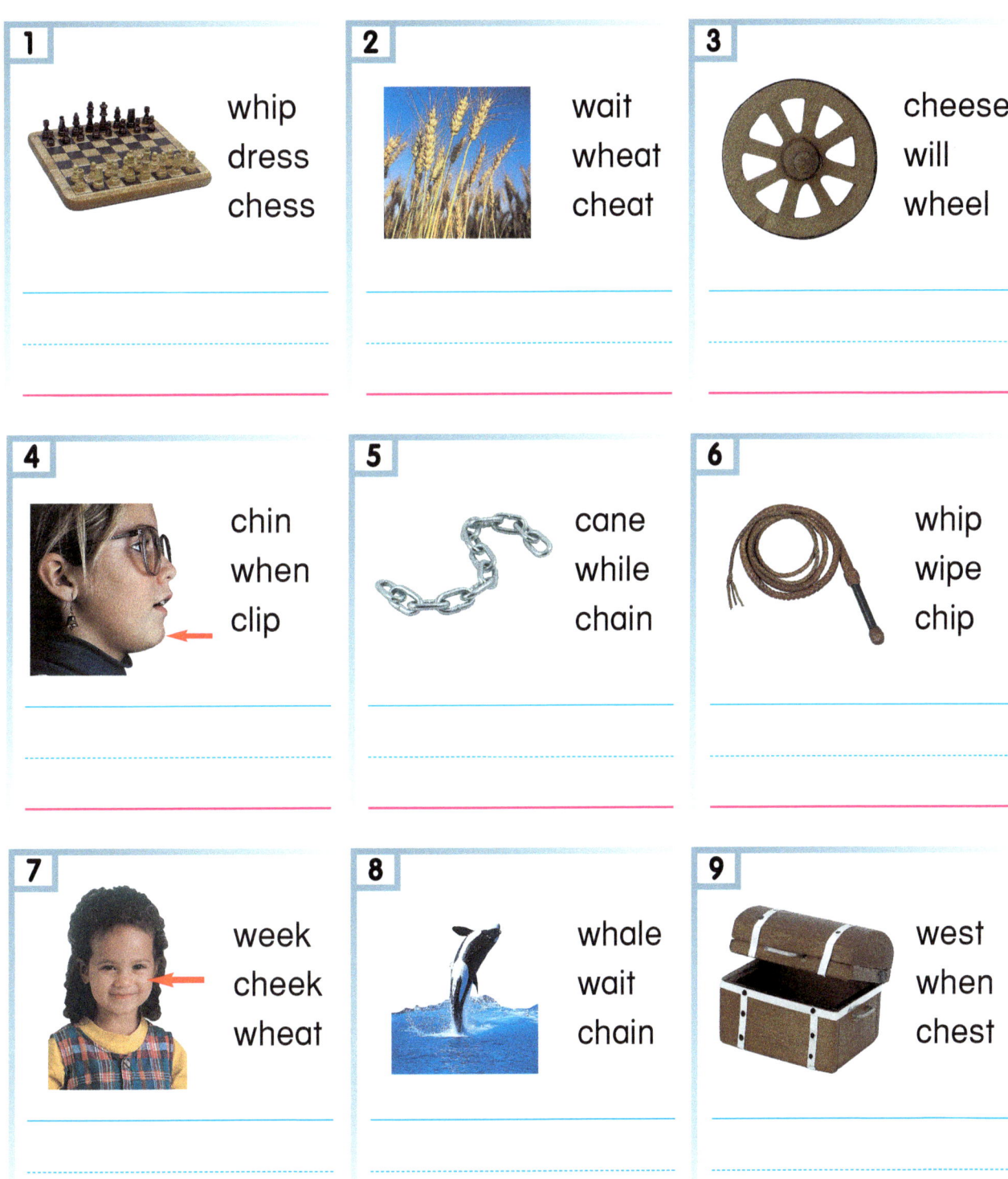

**Circle the word that names the picture.
Write the word.**

1. chip / ship / thin

2. shed / shell / thin

3. spell / then / shell

4. tub / thumb / shut

5. cheap / sheep / she

6. skate / brave / shave

7. shark / spark / third

8. train / short / thorn

9. think / thirty / shirt

Unit 7: Initial Consonant Digraphs
th, *sh*

Point to a picture. Have your child read the picture name and spell the first two letters.

brush   sock

Brush ends with **sh**. **Sock** ends with **ck**. Say each picture name. Listen to the last sound in the word. Write the two letters that stand for the **last** sound.

1. fi
2. sa
3. chi
4. tru
5. clo
6. di
7. bla
8. lea
9. du

Point to a picture. Have your child read the picture name and find another picture name that ends with the same sound.

Unit 7: Final Consonant Digraphs *sh*, *ck*

ring   sink

Ring ends with **ng**. **Sink** ends with **nk**. Say each picture name. Listen to the last sound in the word. Write the two letters that stand for the **last** sound.

1. si___
2. dri___
3. bu___
4. pi___
5. swi___
6. tru___
7. fa___
8. ba___
9. sku___

Unit 7: Final Consonant Digraphs *ng*, *nk*

Say each picture name. Write the missing first and last letters in each word.

PHONICS and SPELLING

1. cloth
2. _u_
3. _u_
4. _i_
5. _i_
6. _o_
7. _u_
8. _i_
9. _a_

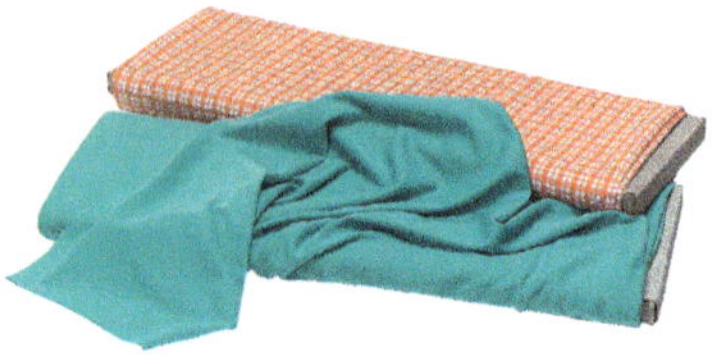

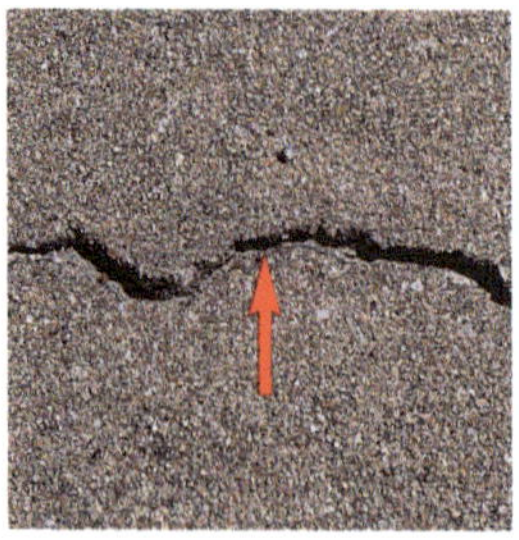

140   Unit 7: Spelling Words with Consonant Blends and Digraphs

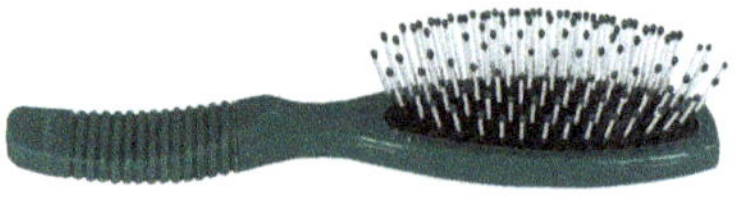

Look at the picture and read the sentence. Circle the word that completes the sentence. Write the word on the line.

PHONICS and READING

1. Patch thinks she can _____.
   sink   sick   sing

2. She sings for _____ in the kitchen.
   chase   cheese   chimp

3. She sings for fish at _____.
   lunch   luck   lamp

4. She sings for a _____ of milk.
   dash   dish   ding

5. Her singing is _____ too loud!
   much   sock   such

6. I _____ she would just purr.
   wing   wish   wink

Ask your child to read the sentences. Then ask your child to find words that end with **sh**, **ch**, and **ng**.

Unit 7: Reading Consonant Digraphs in Context

141

Make believe that you are in space. Write about it. The words in the box may help you.

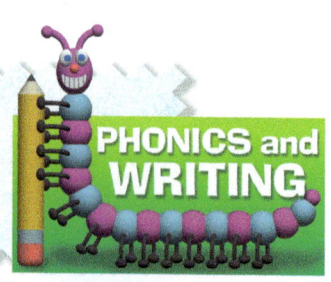

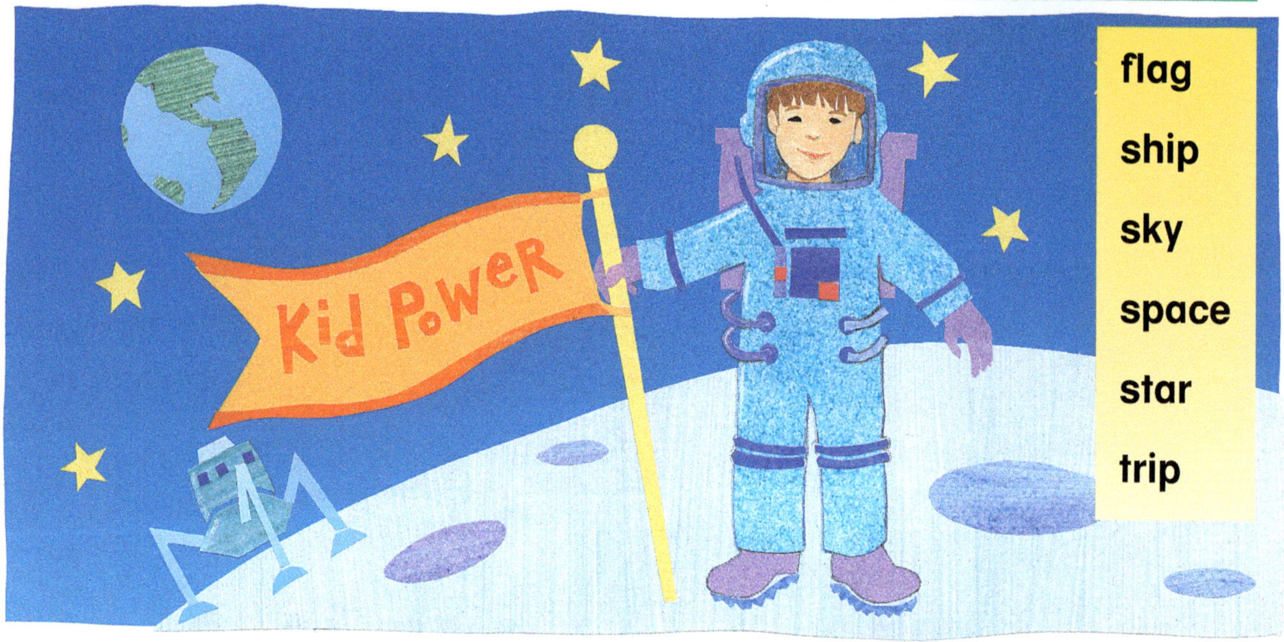

flag
ship
sky
space
star
trip

Circle the word that names the picture. Write the word.

Unit 7 CHECK-UP

1. skunk / trunk
2. tack / tank
3. them / thumb
4. track / black
5. snake / flake
6. crash / crack
7. pink / pinch
8. trick / chick
9. wheel / steel

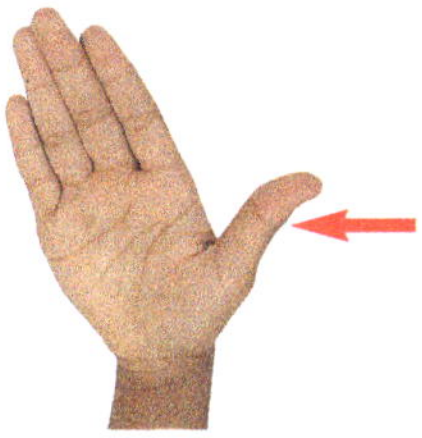

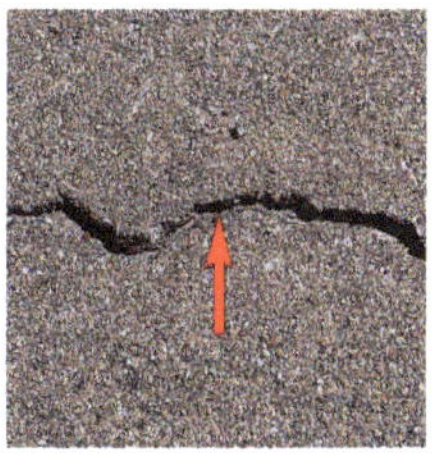

Unit 7: Assessing Consonant Blends and Digraphs

Unit 7 CHECK-UP

Say the picture name. Fill in the circle next to the picture name.

1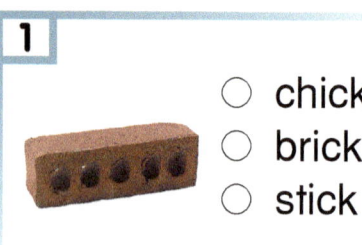
○ chick
○ brick
○ stick

2
○ ring
○ rink
○ rich

3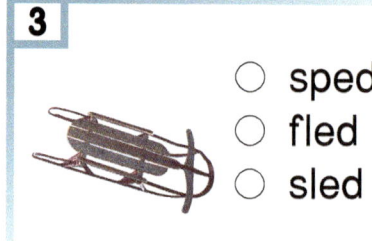
○ sped
○ fled
○ sled

4
○ bank
○ bath
○ bash

5
○ shock
○ block
○ clock

6
○ stain
○ train
○ chain

7
○ crate
○ plate
○ skate

8
○ chill
○ grill
○ spill

9
○ path
○ pack
○ peach

10
○ brush
○ bring
○ broth

11
○ song
○ sock
○ sank

12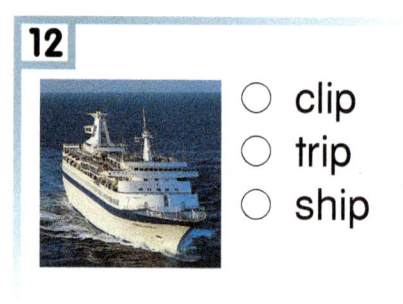
○ clip
○ trip
○ ship

13
○ fog
○ frog
○ drop

14
○ beach
○ back
○ bunk

15
○ skin
○ grin
○ twins